Noodle Soup

by Debbie Caffrey

Debbie's Creative Moments
P.O. Box 70
La Joya, NM 87028-0070

www.debbiescreativemoments.com

Acknowledgements

Thank you to my new long arm machine quilting friends in New Mexico. Phyllis Kent of Los Lunas, New Mexico, quilted *Florida*, *Pajama Party*, *Noodle Soup*, and both of the *Album* quilts. Vel Saddington of Albuquerque, New Mexico, quilted *March Winds*, *Kaleidoscope*, and *Lost Ships*.

Thank you to my long-time friend Karen Tomczak of Anchorage, Alaska, for quilting *Basket Weave*. She is a very talented quilter and a great source of encouragement.

Credits

Photographed by

Pat Berrett
Albuquerque, New Mexico

Printed by

Palmer Printing
St. Cloud, Minnesota

Illustrated by

Debbie Caffrey

Proofread by

Erin Caffrey

Dedication

To my new vice-president, chief financial officer, head of the shipping department, and person-in-charge of everything else I don't want to do, my husband Dan. So this is retirement?

Noodle Soup

Published by

Debbie's Creative Moments
P. O. Box 70
La Joya, NM 87028-0070
USA

ISBN: 0-9645777-5-5

First Printing, 2001

Table of Contents

What is a Noodle?

And, what does it have to do with quilting?

A *noodle* is a strip of fabric that is two inches wide. Strips are cut across the width of the fabric, making them approximately 42" long with selvages on each of the short ends.

How did I happen to come to that definition? It all began with an untitled mystery quilt which required many two-inch-wide strips. After cutting the strips, I looked down at the table and those strips reminded me of the way my grandmother left homemade noodles on the kitchen table to dry. That quilt was named *Noodle Soup*, and so began a series of quilts made from "noodles".

This book follows last year's book *Open a Can of Worms*, in which all of the quilts are constructed using strips that are two and a half inches wide.

Many thoughts led to these books. First of all, there is the popularity of fabric exchanges. I read in many magazines about the desire to exchange 5" or 6" charm squares. I guess I am just too impatient to work with such small pieces, and I refuse keep track of them. Instead, I prefer to gather with friends, cut strips from a yard of several different fabrics, and exchange those. Strip exchanges are a great activity for quilt groups and guilds. I hear that there are some rowdy quilters out there who play their version of strip poker using fabric strips in place of chips or money. If poker is not your game try bingo, trivia games, or some other competition.

Secondly, friendship quilts are quite popular. The quilts in this book are very conducive to making group quilts. With the donation of a few strips from everyone involved, the quilt is finished quickly, and it represents a part of each participant.

Lastly, quilters in my workshops often ask me how I deal with small lengths of fabric in my stash. I realized that rarely do I find the small pieces that are sandwiched in between larger pieces of yardage. What do they get used for anyway? Scrap quilts! By cutting the leftovers into strips the fabrics are in an organized state and ready for a project.

Then came a great revelation. I became aware of triangle tools that would allow me to cut triangles and trapezoids from strips of fabric. A whole new dimension was added to the shapes I could extract from my strips.

It goes without saying that I am really excited about this concept. Not only does it get you organized, but your quilts become more interesting. Consider this: A pattern asks for a dozen strips (noodles) of green. The easy way is to use a piece of one fabric and cut the strips. But, fabric lover that I am, I would really rather have one strip each of twelve different fabrics. Now I just get my box of green noodles and pull out a dozen strips. What could be easier?

Oh, and remember those fabulous fabrics that you had to have? You know, the ones that when you looked at them a few months later you wondered what possessed you to buy them in the first place? Cut them up and you will remember why. Some of the fabrics I cut from my stash had copyright dates from the eighties. What am I saving them for?

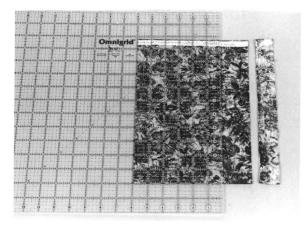

photo #1

General Instructions

It is very important to take the time to review the general instructions prior to using the patterns. Many of the questions that can arise by going directly to the construction of the quilts will be answered in this chapter.

Fabric Yardage & Preparation

Except for the noodles, which obviously have no excess yardage allowance, fabric yardage is fairly generous allowing for shrinkage, straightening, and minor goofs.

I prefer to wash and press my fabrics prior to using them. I began this habit when I first started quilting, and if for no other reason, I continue to wash them because I do not care to use washed and unwashed fabrics together in the same project. I have made quilts using only new, unwashed fabric, and I have to say I did not like handling the fabrics.

To avoid distorting your fabric as you press the yardage, move your iron in strokes that are parallel to the selvages. This is in the direction of the stable warp yarns that do not stretch with the iron's strokes. Too often I had quilters come to class with fabrics that seem to have wavy, wobbly edges along the selvages. Most of the time this problem is not due to the quality of the fabric. It is created by moving the iron from side to side between the selvages while applying any combination of the following: heavy pressure, steam, and starch or sizing.

Steam, starch, and sizing are fine, but take care that you do not distort the fabric. Some patterns will require you to sew along the bias edges of triangles and trapezoids. Spray starching your fabrics prior to cutting them will help stabilize them against stretching as you sew.

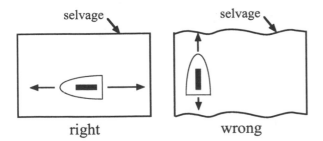

right   wrong

Cutting

The quilts in this book are all designed for rotary cutting and machine piecing. Most of you are quite familiar with your rotary cutter. With that in mind, you may be surprised that I have elected to talk about strip cutting. This is the information that quilters in my workshops call "worth the price of admission".

When cutting strips for a project, I use my 15" square ruler. The same technique can be used with most square rulers that are 12" or larger.

Begin by folding your fabric in half, selvage to selvage. Fold it in half a second time, matching the fold to the selvages.

> **HINT:** Instead of wrestling with long lengths of fabric (more than a yard and a half or so), I estimate how much I need and cut off a piece that is slightly longer. For instance, if I need to cut six to eight 2" wide strips, I cut off a half yard, press it, and use that for cutting the strips.

After folding the fabric in preparation for strip cutting, square off one end, removing the uneven edge. Rotate your mat a half turn or walk to the opposite side of the table to begin cutting the strips. Do not turn only the fabric. That will disturb the even edge.

Let us assume that you need to cut many noodles (you know, 2" wide strips). Most of you line up the 2" line of a ruler with the square edge of the fabric and cut a strip. Then, you move the ruler off the strip, move the strip, reposition the ruler to cut the next strip, move the ruler off the strip, move the strip, etc. After doing this four or five times, you check your strip and find that there are bends in it that make the strip resemble a "W". So, it is back to the beginning (and the other side of the table) to square the edge again. The reason that strips have these bends at the folds is that the edge from which you are measuring gets "out of square" by having the ruler tilted an unnoticeable amount with each cut. These tilts compound and cause crooked strips.

Instead of that old routine, consider this. Using your 15" ruler, you can cut seven 2" strips very quickly and more accurately. Start by placing the 14" line of the ruler on the squared edge of the folded fabric. You now have seven 2" strips under your ruler. Granted, the fabric is not cut into strips yet, but it will be in a minute.

Don't move any of the fabric or strips as you cut them. This is just wasted motion. With the vertical 14" line of the ruler on the squared edge of the fabric and any of the horizontal lines of the ruler along the lower fold of the fabric, cut. See figure 1 below. This procedure results in a very square cut and enough fabric under the ruler to cut the seven 2" wide strips.

Next, slide the ruler to the left until the 12" line is on the squared end of the fabric. That exposes a 2" strip of fabric between the cut you just made and the edge of the ruler. Make sure that a horizontal line of the ruler is still along the lower fold of the fabric and cut. See figure 2 on the next page.

Slide the ruler to the left another 2" inches and align the 10" line with the squared end of the fabric. Another 2" of fabric is exposed. Check to see that a horizontal line is on the lower fold of the fabric and cut. See figure 3 on the next page.

Continue sliding the ruler to the left 2" at a time and making cuts until all seven strips have been cut. At that time, stack and remove the strips. If you need more strips for your project, repeat these steps until all the strips are cut. There should be no need to square and straighten the end of the fabric unless you disturb it while repositioning it on the cutting mat.

Use this method even when you are cutting fewer strips. Start with a different line. For example, if you have only seven inches of fabric remaining, align the 6" line with the squared edge of the fabric. There are three uncut 2" wide strips under your ruler. Cut along the edge of the ruler. After cutting, move the ruler 2" to the left to the 4" line for the second cut, and so on.

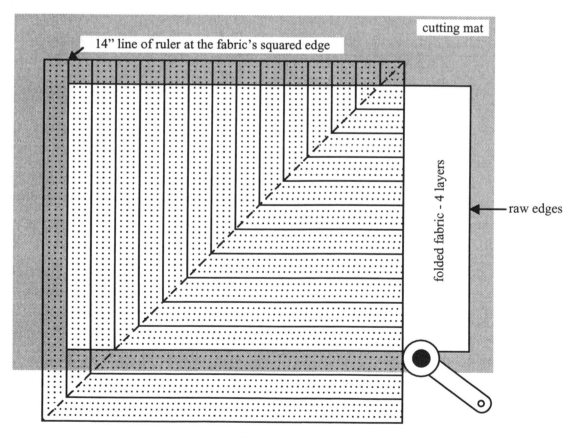

fig. 1

6

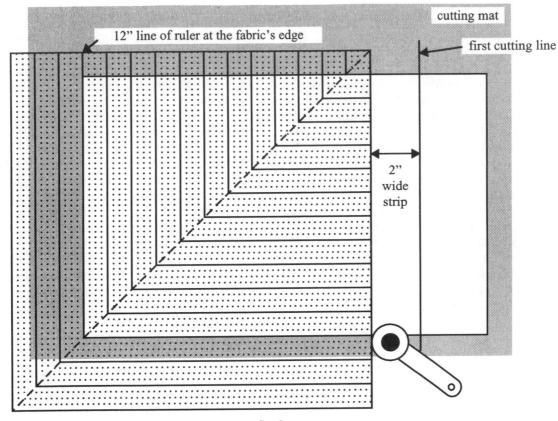

cutting mat

12" line of ruler at the fabric's edge

first cutting line

2" wide strip

fig. 2

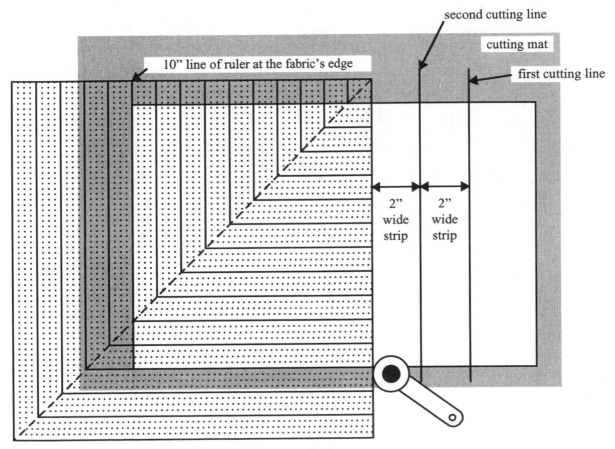

second cutting line

cutting mat

10" line of ruler at the fabric's edge

first cutting line

2" wide strip

2" wide strip

fig. 3

Consider another example. Let us say that for another project you need to cut strips that are 2 1/4" wide. Take the time to list your "target numbers". Target numbers for the 2" wide strips are 14", 12", 10", 8", 6", 4", and 2". Make a chart of your target numbers for the new size (multiples of 2 1/4" for this example) that reads as such: 13 1/2", 11 1/4", 9", 6 3/4", 4 1/2", and 2 1/4".

This means that when you align the ruler with the squared edge of the fabric to make your first cut, you will use the 13 1/2" line. Thirteen and a half inches will yield six 2 1/4" strips. Continue moving the ruler and cutting as directed for the 2" wide strips, but use the target numbers from above so that you are cutting 2 1/4" wide strips.

This same principle of cutting can be applied to crosscutting strips into squares and rectangles. Figure 4 at the bottom of this page demonstrates cutting a 2" strip into 2" squares.

To do so, open the folded strip to two layers instead of four. If you feel brave enough, neatly stack four folded strips on top of each other so that you can cut through eight layers at a time. Trim the selvages, squaring that end. Crosscut the strip(s) into squares as previously directed for cutting strips. If necessary, reposition the strip to cut squares from the remainder.

Use this method of cutting for crosscutting strip pieced panels, such as those in the *March Winds* quilt on page 44. It will save lots of time and improve your precision.

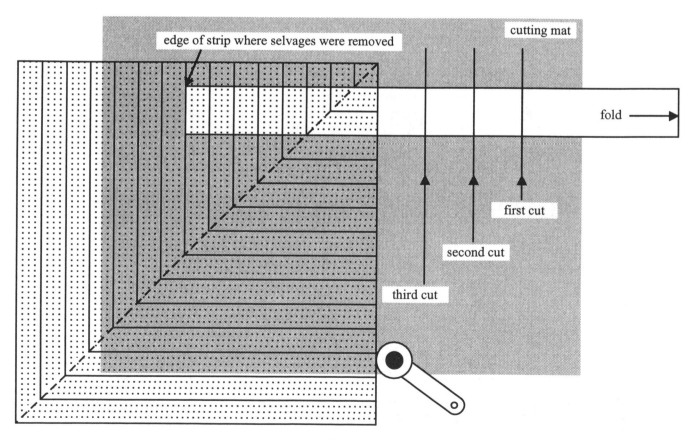

edge of strip where selvages were removed

cutting mat

fold

first cut

second cut

third cut

fig. 4

Crosscutting Strip-Pieced Panels

The diagrams below and on the next page (figures 5 and 6), show you how to stack the strip-pieced panels from the *March Winds* pattern, preparing to crosscut them into 2" wide sections.

For this technique you will need to use the gridded side of your cutting mat. Align the top of the first panel with a grid line to make sure it is straight. Match the top edge of the second panel to the seam line of the first panel. Match the top edge of the third panel to the seam line of the second panel, and match the top edge of the fourth panel to the seam line of the third panel. See figure 6 on the next page. Add a fifth and perhaps a sixth panel in the same fashion.

Crosscut the sections using a 15" square, starting at the 14" line, as directed for crosscutting squares on the previous page. See photos 2 and 3 on the next page.

Using the Templates

When using templates, I take the easy way out. I use a copy machine or my computer to make templates. *Be sure to compare copies to the original!!! Many copiers greatly distort and your templates may be incorrect.*

Tape the templates to the underside of any suitable tool that you have using double sided tape. See photos 6, 7, and 8 on pages 65 and 68. I prefer to use a temporary adhesive. Check for it at your local craft or office supply store. Use these set-ups just as you would the various triangle tools.

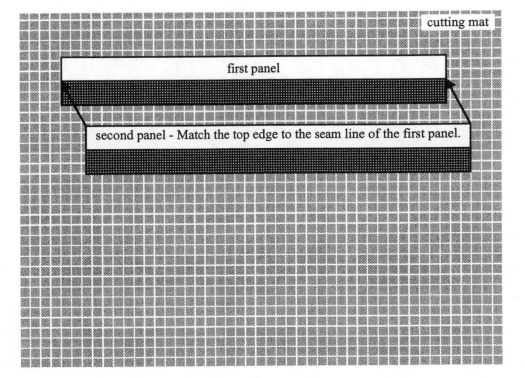

fig. 5

9

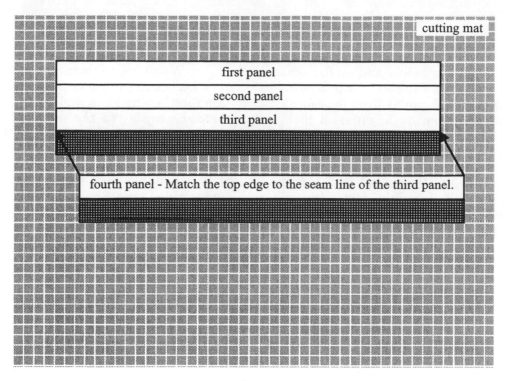

first panel

second panel

third panel

fourth panel - Match the top edge to the seam line of the third panel.

cutting mat

fig. 6

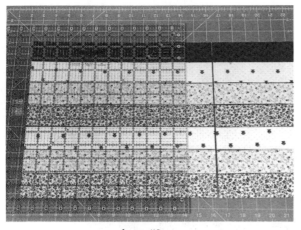

photo #2   photo #3

Sewing Precision

The success of your quilts depends upon precise seam allowances. *I cannot stress this point enough.* Do not believe the person who tells you that as long as you are consistent, it will be okay. That only works for a few quilts, like *Basket Weave* and similar ones. Quilts that have areas of many seams as well as other areas with few seams must be constructed with accurate seam allowances. If you have not checked your seam allowances in the past, do so by performing the following test.

Test: From scraps cut four rectangles that measure 1 1/2" x 4 1/2". Sew them together along the long edges using a scant 1/4" seam allowance. This is about a needle's width narrower than a true 1/4".

Press the seam allowances to one side. The finished piece should measure 4 1/2" square. If not, adjust your seam allowance and repeat the test.

The finished sample will measure 4 1/2" square.

10

Borders

The outer border strips should be cut with the lengthwise grain in the long direction whenever possible. This will keep the borders from stretching and rippling. The yardage requirements allow for lengthwise grain borders. It is not necessary that narrow inner borders be cut along the lengthwise grain.

My solution to cutting accurate, long, lengthwise grain border strips is summed up in one word -- tear! Tearing is recommended for 100% cotton fabrics, only. Test fabrics of other fiber content before tearing the yardage.

Fabrics are woven with the strong warp yarns running in the lengthwise direction and the weaker weave yarns in the crosswise direction. This is the very reason why the fabric doesn't stretch along the lengthwise grain while having a good deal of give on the crosswise grain. When tearing across the width of fabrics, you are breaking the stronger yarns, which leads to snags and weakening of the fabric beyond the 1/4" seam allowances.

On the other hand, when tearing fabric along its length, you are breaking the weak yarns and tearing parallel to the warp yarns. The result is a much smoother edge and a perfectly straight, on-grain border strip.

If you are unsure about how well your fabric will tear, start by tearing off a selvage. Clip one end of the fabric 1" away from the selvage edge. Tear this selvage off. Do not be timid. Pull firmly and rather quickly. What do you think of the edge? Press the torn edge. How does it look now? If it is satisfactory, you are ready to tear the borders.

Lay an end of the border fabric flat on a table. Measure the desired cut width of your border from the edge where you have removed the selvage. See figure 7. Make a clip at this point on the end of the fabric just as you did when removing the selvage. Measure from this first clip and make a second clip for the second border. Repeat to mark all four borders. Tear!

Press the border strips. I prewash my fabrics before piecing a quilt. I do not press the border fabric until it is torn into strips. A narrow strip of fabric is easier to press than yards of the full width fabric.

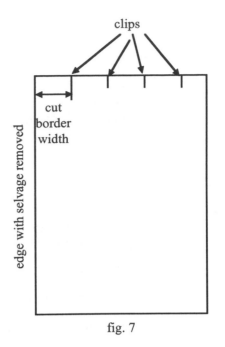

fig. 7

Measuring and easing are important steps. Without them your quilt may be different lengths on opposite sides and will not be square. Be sure the quilt is pressed well before measuring it. As you are measuring, keep the quilt top fairly taut on a flat surface. The quilt top contains many seams, and they each have a slight amount of slack where the seam allowances are pressed to the side. Conversely, the borders have few or no seams and are cut along the stable, lengthwise grain. Therefore, keeping the quilt taut while measuring is imperative, but do not stretch quilts that are set on point.

Borders can be applied with either overlapped or mitered corners. *If you choose to miter the borders for any of the quilts in these patterns, purchase an additional half yard of border fabric.* The amount of fabric allowed is for overlapped borders.

Overlapped Corners

Find the length of the quilt. Measure in several places to determine the average length. Take measurements along seam lines and in areas that go through the centers of the blocks, but not along the outside edges. Cut two border strips 1/2" wider than the desired finished width of the border by the average measured length of the quilt.

Pin the borders to the sides of the

quilt, matching the center points and ends of the quilt and borders. Continue pinning the borders to the quilt, easing if necessary. Sew. Press the seam allowances toward the borders.

Now, determine the width of the quilt, measuring in several places, as before. Include the additional width created by the side borders. Cut two border strips to fit (finished border width plus 1/2" x width of quilt) and pin them to the top and bottom of the quilt as you did the side borders. Sew. Press the seam allowances toward the borders. See figure 8.

If you are adding more than one border, repeat the above steps for each one.

fig. 8
quilt with overlapped borders

Mitered Corners

The only quilt in this book with mitered corners is *Lost Ships*. Depending upon the fabric you choose, you may want to miter the corners of the borders in other quilts. Mitered corners require 1/2 yard more fabric on the average than do overlapped corners.

Determine both the width and length of your quilt. To calculate how long to cut your borders, add two times the border width plus an inch or two to the measurements of your quilt. If the quilt will have more than one border with mitered corners, sew the borders together into a panel before attaching them.

Even with mitered corners you can square your quilt. Put a pin at the center of each border. Measure half the length of your quilt in each direction from the center pin and mark those points with pins. Now, pin the border to your quilt, matching the pins with the center and ends of the quilt. Use additional pins as needed.

Attach borders to two opposite sides of the quilt first. Begin and end the stitching on the seam line, 1/4" from the edge of the quilt top. Backstitch at each end. See figure 9. Press the seam allowances toward the borders. Repeat with the remaining two border pieces.

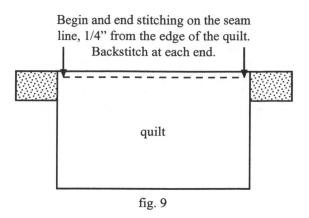

Begin and end stitching on the seam line, 1/4" from the edge of the quilt. Backstitch at each end.

quilt

fig. 9

Place a corner of the quilt on the ironing board. Lay the vertical border on the ironing board first. Lay the horizontal border over it, as shown. See figure 10.

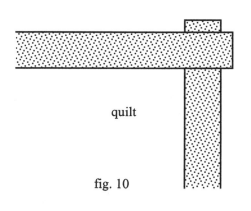

quilt

fig. 10

Tuck the end of the horizontal border under so that the fold makes a 45 degree angle. See figure 11. Press. Lay a ruler on top of this corner to check that it is square and the angle is accurate. If your border is strip pieced, make sure the seam lines match.

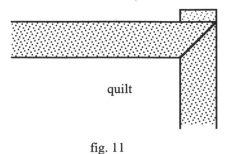

quilt

fig. 11

Place the borders right sides together and pin. Match the seam lines if the borders have more than one fabric. Stitch on the pressed crease, starting on the seam line, being careful not to catch the quilt top in the stitching. Stitch to the outer edge of the border. Check your work. Make sure you are pleased with the finished corner before doing any trimming. If it is correct, trim the excess fabric, leaving 1/4" for seam allowances. Press the seam allowances to one side or open. Repeat this process for all four corners.

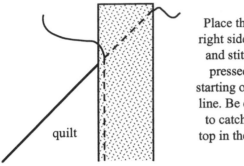

Place the borders right sides together and stitch on the pressed crease, starting on the seam line. Be careful not to catch the quilt top in the stitching.

Quilting and Binding

These basic skills have books and classes dedicated solely to them. Almost every quilting magazine on the market contains basic instruction for quilting and binding in every issue. Take advantage of demonstrations and classes that are available to you. The quilting and binding are highly visible and are a part of every quilt. Learn to do them well.

If you need more detailed information for binding, *Happy Endings*, by Mimi Dietrich, published by That Patchwork Place, is a good reference.

After quilting, trim the excess batting and backing in preparation for binding. I use a 1/2" wide binding. Many quilts have pieced edges, and therefore, have only 1/4" seam allowances. To allow for the 1/2" binding, trim the backing and batting, leaving an additional 1/4" beyond the raw edge of the quilt top. This will create the necessary 1/2" seam allowance.

For a 1/2" double binding, cut cross-grain strips 3 1/4" wide. Bias strips are only necessary for binding curves. Although, some fabrics, like plaids and stripes, make a more interesting binding when cut on the bias. Cut enough strips to go around the perimeter of your quilt. Sew them together, end on end, and press the seam allowances open. Press the binding in half, wrong sides together, lengthwise.

Sew the binding to the quilt with 1/2" seam allowances, aligning the raw edges of the binding with the cut edge of the quilt. Start in the middle of one side, *leaving the first six inches of binding unsewn*. Stitch, stopping 1/2" from the corner. Lift your presser foot and pull the quilt out a few inches from under the machine to fold the binding. It is not necessary to clip the threads. Rotate the quilt a quarter turn, counterclockwise. Fold the binding up and away, creating a 45 degree angle. Then, fold the binding back down toward you.

Begin stitching at the edge of the quilt. Continue stitching down the second side, stopping 1/2" from the corner. Miter this corner as you did the first one and continue around the quilt. After you have mitered the last corner, *stop stitching 12" from where you first began to attach the binding*.

Trim the excess binding, leaving 1/4" on each end for seam allowances. Stitch the two ends of the binding together. Press the seam allowances open. Finish stitching this section of the binding to the quilt.

Push the binding to the back of the quilt and pin in place. The folded edge of the binding should just cover the stitching line. Fold the corners into neat miters on the back of the quilt. Hand stitch the binding into place.

Templates

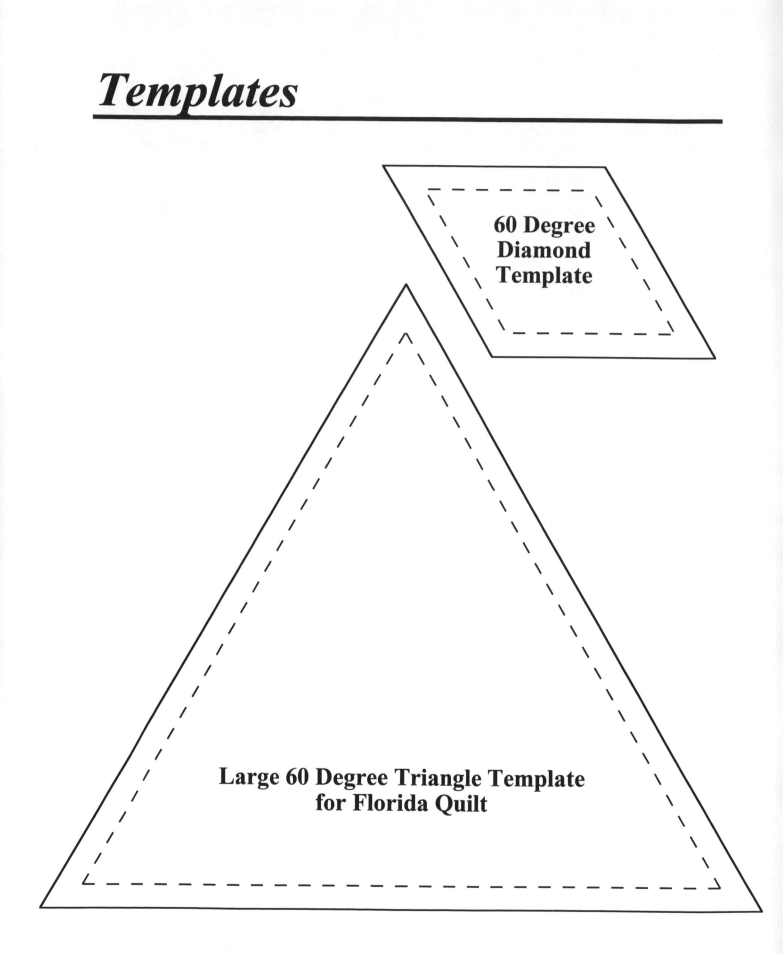

60 Degree Diamond Template

Large 60 Degree Triangle Template for Florida Quilt

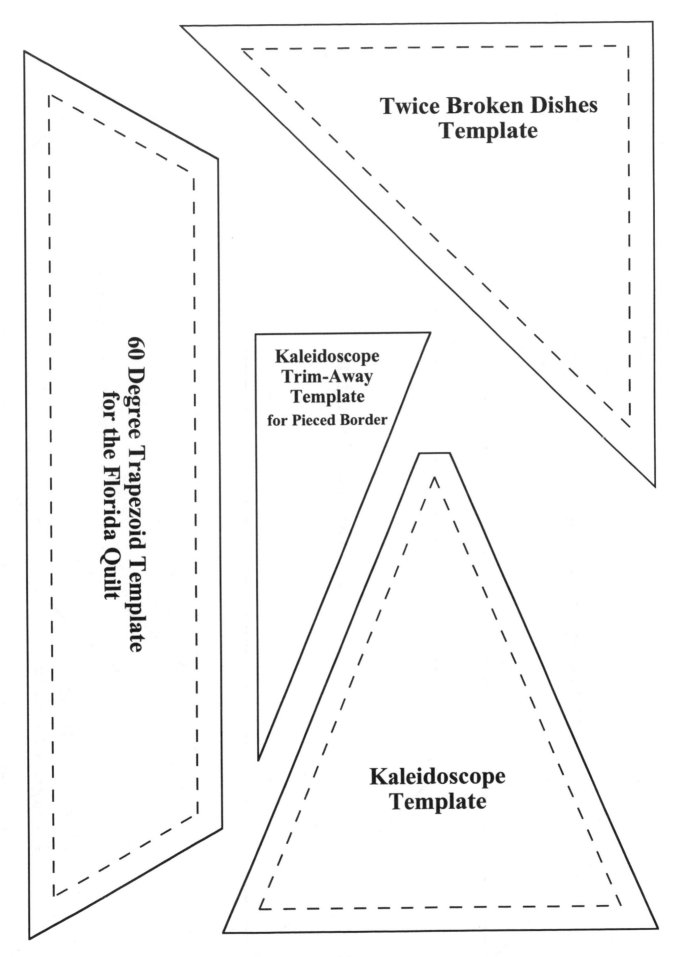

Twice Broken Dishes Template

60 Degree Trapezoid Template for the Florida Quilt

Kaleidoscope Trim-Away Template
for Pieced Border

Kaleidoscope Template

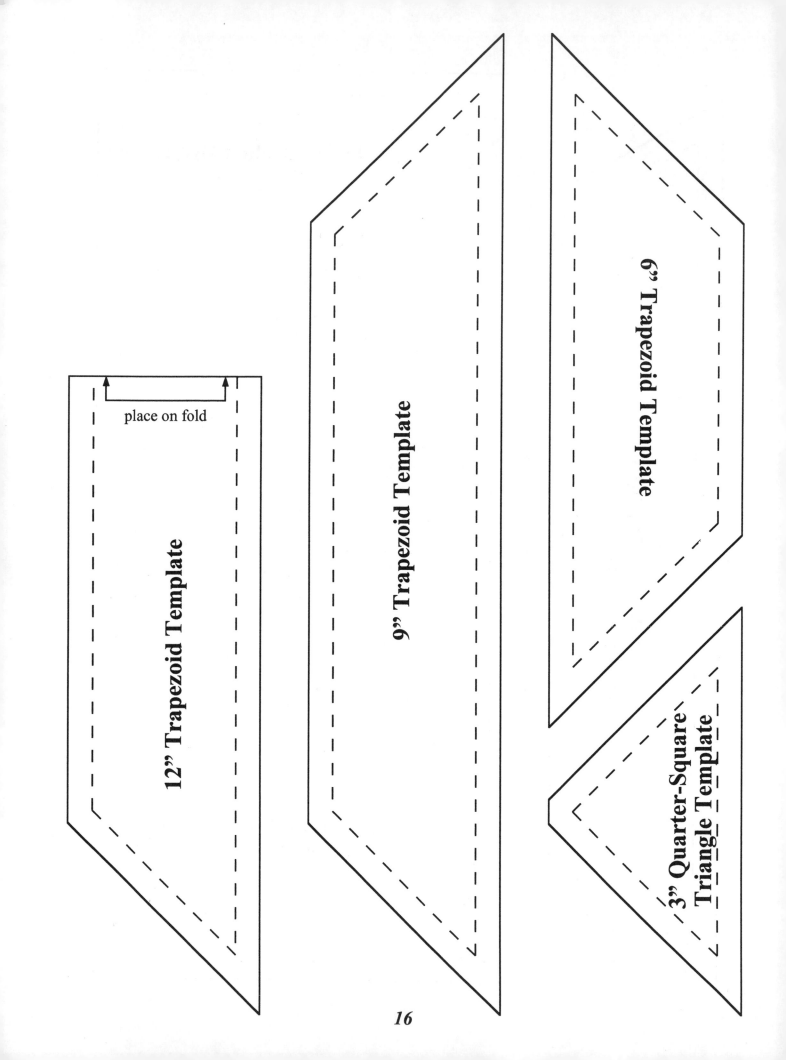

place on fold

12" Trapezoid Template

9" Trapezoid Template

6" Trapezoid Template

3" Quarter-Square Triangle Template

Noodle Soup -- 81" x 102"

Pieced by Debbie Caffrey and Quilted by Phyllis Kent of Los Lunas, New Mexico

Doll Houses -- 43" x 43"

Pieced and Quilted by Debbie Caffrey

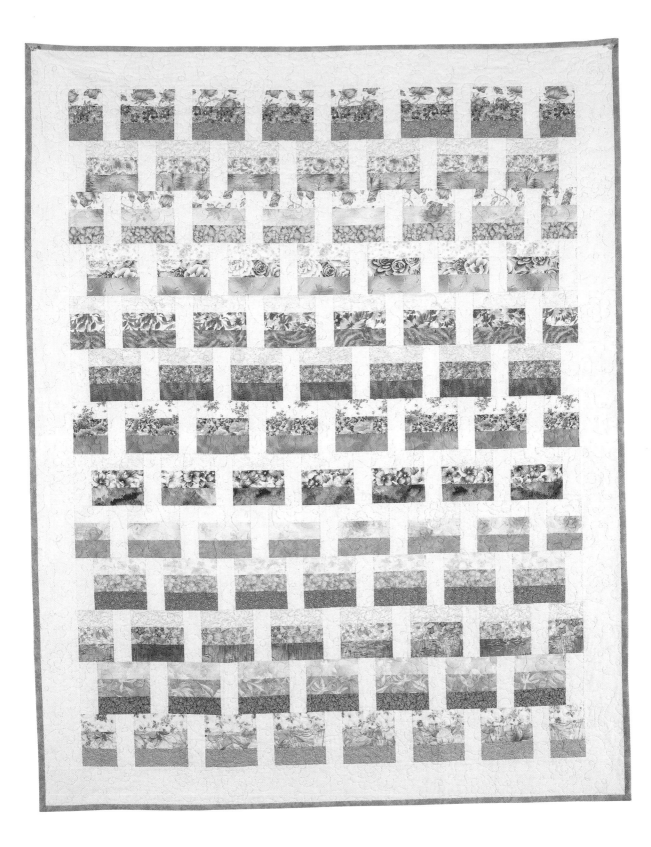

Basket Weave -- 51 1/2" x 64 1/2"

Pieced by Debbie Caffrey and Quilted by Karen Tomczak of Anchorage, Alaska

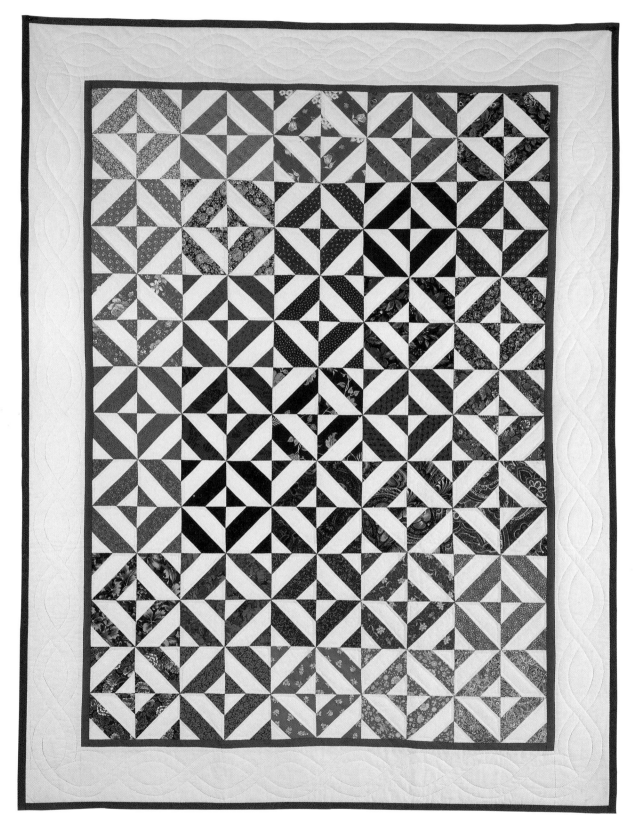

Twice Broken Dishes -- 52" x 68"

Pieced and Hand Quilted by Debbie Caffrey

Florida Quilt -- 55 1/2" x 71"

Pieced by Debbie Caffrey and Quilted by Phyllis Kent of Los Lunas, New Mexico

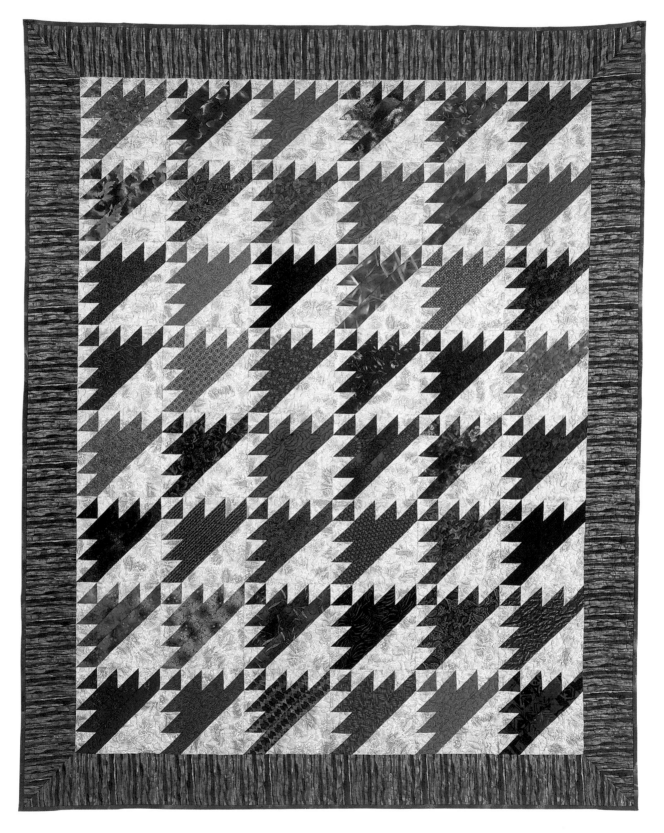

Lost Ships -- 62" x 79"

Pieced by Debbie Caffrey and Quilted by Vel Saddington of Albuquerque, New Mexico

Kaleidoscope -- 58" x 58"

Pieced by Debbie Caffrey and Quilted by Vel Saddington of Albuquerque, New Mexico

Album Quilt / Row Assembly -- 57 1/2" x 68"

Pieced by Debbie Caffrey and Quilted by Phyllis Kent of Los Lunas, New Mexico

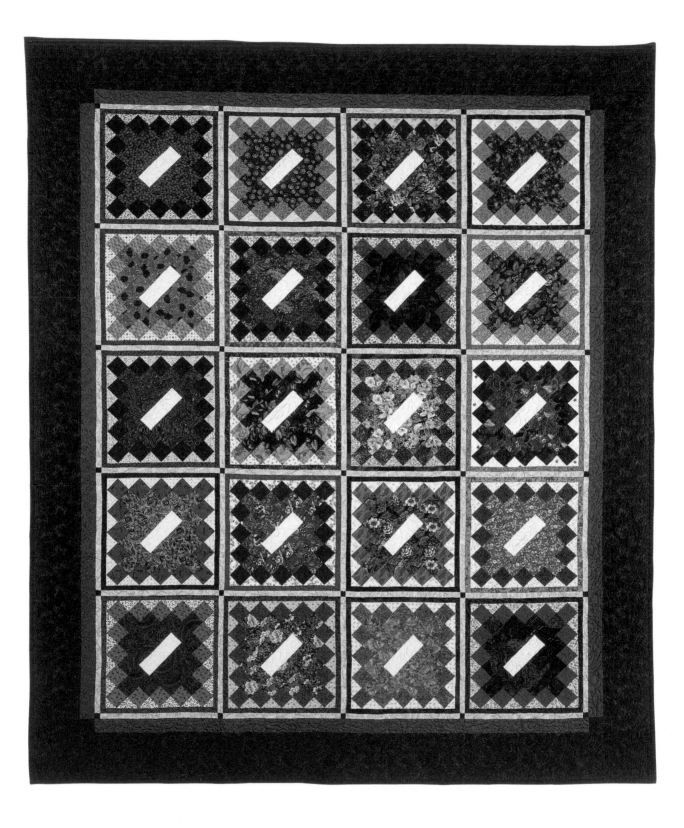

Album Quilt / Block Assembly -- 62" x 74"

Pieced by Debbie Caffrey and Quilted by Phyllis Kent of Los Lunas, New Mexico

Liberty Stars -- 45" x 55 1/2"

Pieced and Quilted by Debbie Caffrey

Pajama Party -- 46 1/2" x 61"

Pieced by Debbie Caffrey and Quilted by Phyllis Kent of Los Lunas, New Mexico

March Winds -- 64" x 76"

Pieced by Debbie Caffrey and Quilted by Vel Saddington of Albuquerque, New Mexico

Basket Weave

The size of the quilt shown on page 19 is 51 1/2" x 64 1/2".

Fabric Requirements

Select your strips in sets of three. The three strips in each set will be used to make one strip-pieced panel, and each panel will make one horizontal row of the quilt. Each set should contain one light, one medium, and one dark strip. The fabrics of the three strips in each panel should create a pleasing movement from one to the next. See the photograph on page 19 for some examples.

39 noodles (thirteen each of light, medium, and dark)

Sashing & borders (white or other)	**1 3/4 yards**
Binding	**3/4 yard**
Backing	**3 1/4 yards**

Cutting

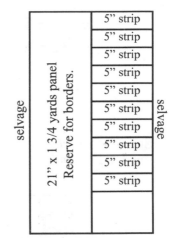

Sashing

Cut a 21" wide x 1 3/4 yards long panel from the sashing and border fabric. Reserve this for the borders.

From the remaining fabric
Cut ten 5" wide strips.
    Cut these strips into ninety-seven 2" x 5" rectangles.

Piecing

Sew the thirteen sets of three strips into panels, placing the medium value in the center of each panel. Press the seam allowances toward the dark.

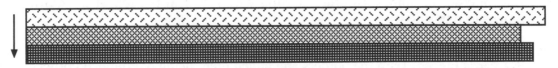

make 13 panels

Arrange the panels as horizontal rows in a pleasing order. Number the rows from 1 to 13, starting at the top and continuing to the bottom.

Crosscut each of the panels for the *even* rows into seven 5" wide sections.

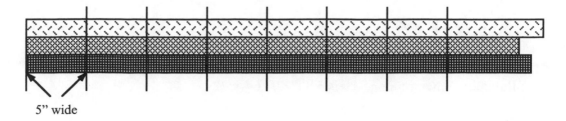

5" wide

Sew each *even* row together, placing a 2" x 5" sashing rectangle between each block and at each end, as shown below. Press the seam allowances toward the sashing.

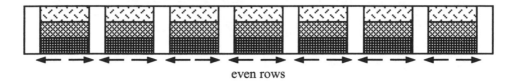

even rows

Crosscut each of the panels for the *odd* rows into six 5" wide sections and two 3 1/2" wide sections.

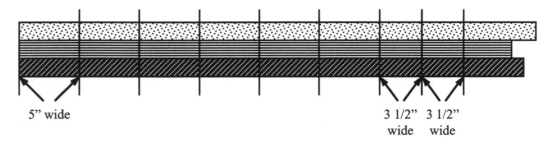

5" wide

3 1/2"   3 1/2"
wide   wide

Sew each *odd* row together, placing a 2" x 5" sashing rectangle between each block, and using the 3 1/2" blocks on the ends, as shown below. Press the seam allowances toward the sashing.

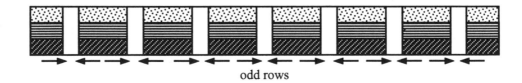

odd rows

Sew the rows together in numerical order starting with row 1 at the top of the quilt. Press the seam allowances to one side.

Trim the selvage from the reserved panel of border fabric. Split the panel lengthwise into four 4 1/2" x 1 3/4 yards pieces. Trim the borders and attach them using overlapped corners. See page 11 for more instruction on borders.

Options to Consider --

Full or Queen Size

A full/queen size quilt would require two 2" wide strips of each fabric to make longer rows so the quilt will be wide enough. In addition, it will require nineteen (full size) or twenty-one (queen size) rows. That means the full size quilt will use thirty-eight strips (two each of nineteen fabrics) of light and the same number for the medium and dark fabrics, making a total of 114 strips, two each of fifty-seven fabrics. The queen size quilt will use forty-two strips (two each of twenty-one fabrics) of light and the same number for the medium and dark fabrics, making a total of 126 strips, two each of sixty-three fabrics.

Sew two panels for each row. Cut the first panel of each set as directed for odd and even rows, respectively. Crosscut the second panel of each set into seven (for a full size) or eight (for a queen size) 5" wide sections.

Purchase four yards of fabric for the border and sashing. Reserve a 20" x 2 3/4 yards piece for the border, and cut 2" x 5" sashes from the remainder. Cut 275 rectangles for the full size and 325 rectangles for the queen size. Add borders as desired.

Another Fabric Placement

Perhaps an easier way to select fabrics for this quilt is to choose three colors.

For example, you could make a quilt with a traditional Americana color scheme by choosing red, white, and blue. Decide how many panels you will need in order to make the size of quilt you desire. Then gather an equal number of strips of different reds, whites, and blues. Make red, white, and blue panels, placing the colors in the same position in each panel.

Crosscut the panels into sections, making sure you have enough 3 1/2" wide sections to complete the ends of the odd rows, and cutting the remainder into 5" wide sections.

Cut the number of 2" x 5" sashes needed to complete the quilt. Mix the blocks and use them randomly as you piece rows.

Noodle Soup Quilt

The size of the quilt shown on page 17 is 81" x 102".

This is the quilt that started it all. It was originally designed as a mystery quilt pattern. Naming mystery quilts without giving away the pattern is often a challenge. When I had finished cutting the many 2" wide strips for making this quilt, I looked at them scattered about on my cutting table. Lying there in a haphazard heap, they reminded me of the times my grandmother made homemade noodles and left them to dry on the kitchen table.

Fabric Requirements

35 medium dark to dark noodles	
Light background fabric	3 yards
Light medium fabric (orchid)	2 1/2 yards
Outer border (blue violet)	2 3/4 yards
Inner border & binding (dark green)	1 3/4 yards
Backing	7 1/2 yards

Cutting

Medium dark to dark noodles

Cut all of the noodles in half to make two 2" x 21" sections from each.
Use four of these sections to cut thirty-two 2" squares.
Reserve the remaining sixty-six sections for strip-piecing.

Light background fabric

Cut five strips 8" wide.
    Cut these strips into seventeen 8" squares and fourteen 5" x 8" rectangles.
Cut five strips 5" wide.
Cut two strips 3 1/2" wide.
    Cut these strips into twenty-eight 2" x 3 1/2" rectangles.
Cut six strips 2" wide.

Light medium fabric

Cut twelve strips 3 1/2" wide.
    Cut these strips into 144 squares (3 1/2").
Cut eleven strips 2" wide.

Inner border

Cut ten strips 2 3/4" wide.
    Use three strips for each side, two strips for the top, and two strips for the bottom.

Piecing

Fold all of the strips of background fabric (both sizes, 2" and 5"), and the 2" strips of light medium fabric in half, selvage to selvage, and cut the folds to make them approximately 21" long.

Sew the strips together to make the following panels. These panels will measure approximately 21" across. Use the various dark noodles randomly. Press the seam allowances in the directions shown by the arrows.

 Background fabric

Light medium

All other patterns symbolize the various dark noodles.

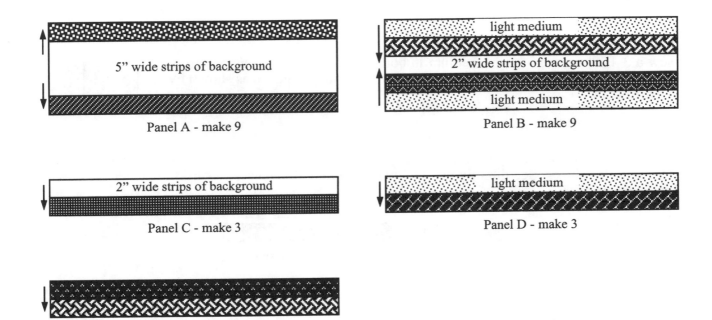

Panel A - make 9

Panel B - make 9

Panel C - make 3

Panel D - make 3

Panel E - make 12

Crosscut *all* of the strip-pieced panels from above into sections that are 2" wide. Stack the panels, if desired, to speed up the process. See page 9 for more details. *Measure and cut carefully. Mistakes are quickly multiplied with the panels stacked.*

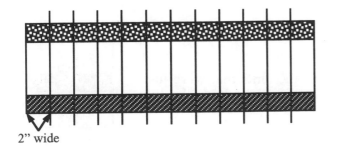

2" wide

A panels	Cut 82 sections.
B panels	Cut 82 sections.
C panels	Cut 28 sections.
D panels	Cut 28 sections.
E panels	Cut 110 sections.

Sew the sections from the C panels to those from the D panels to make twenty-eight four patch units like the one shown at the right. Press the seam allowances to one side.

make 28

Sew a 2" x 3 1/2" rectangle of background fabric to the four patch units from above to make the sections shown at the right. Pay close attention to the positions of the pieces. Make fourteen of each. Press the seam allowances toward the rectangle.

make 14   make 14

Sew the sections from the A panels to those from the B panels to make eighty-two units like the one shown at thc right. Press the seam allowances in the direction shown by the arrow.

make 82

Sew a 3 1/2" square of light medium to both sides of forty-six sections from the E panels. Press the seam allowances toward the large squares as shown by the arrows.

make 46

Sew sections from the E panels to two opposite sides of twenty-eight of the 2" squares of the dark noodle fabrics. See directly below. Press the seam allowances toward the center as shown by the arrows.

⬛ + ⬛ + ⬛ = ⬛⬛⬛⬛

make 28

Sew a ⬛ section to each ⬛ section. Press the seam allowances in the direction shown by the arrow.

make 28

Sew a second ⬛ section to eighteen of the units that were just completed above. Press the seam allowances in the direction shown by the arrow.

make 18

Use four 3 1/2" squares of light medium, eight sections from the E panels, and four of the 2" squares of noodle fabric to make four corner units like the one shown directly at the right. Press the seam allowances in the directions shown.

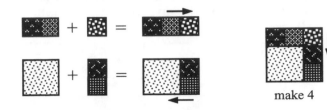

make 4

It is time to assemble the quilt top.

Refer to the exploded diagram on the next page to lay out the quilt.

The remaining 3 1/2" squares of light medium fabric are the cornerstones.

The eighty-two sections are the sashes.

The blocks, six of the partial blocks, all of 8" squares of background, and eight of the 5" x 8" rectangles of background are used to construct the wide rows with forty-two of the sashes.

All other miscellaneous units are used at the ends of the even rows or to make the top and bottom rows.

There are seventeen rows in this quilt. Only four fill patterns are used in the sketch so that it will be easier to identify the pieces and their positions. You may choose to make a four fabric variation instead of the scrappy one. Details follow in the *Options to Consider* section.

HINT: Rows 3, 7, 11, and 15 are exactly alike. Make them all at the same time. Rows 5, 9, and 13 are exactly alike. Make them all at the same time. All of the even rows are exactly alike, too, but every other one is turned upside down to create the pattern. Make the even rows all at the same time. Finally, the top and bottom rows are exactly alike, but the bottom one is turned upside down after construction. Make these two rows at the same time.

Sew the units and blocks into horizontal rows. Press the seam allowances as directed on the next page. Sew the rows together. Press the seam allowances to one side.

Attach inner borders with overlapped corners. Cut the outer border fabric lengthwise into four equal panels. Cut the panels 6 1/2" wide for a full size or 10 1/2" wide for a queen size. Attach them to the quilt. See page 11 for more instruction on borders.

Options to Consider --

Another Fabric Placement

This quilt can be made effectively with four fabrics. Cut twenty-nine 2" wide strips from one medium dark fabric (2 yards). Use two strips to cut thirty-two 2" squares. Use the remaining twenty-seven strips for strip-piecing. Cut six 2" wide strips of a dark fabric (1/2 yard). Use one of these strips and one strip of medium dark when piecing the E panels.

Use the medium dark fabric for the wide outer border. Use the dark fabric for the narrow inner border and the binding.

35

Use this sketch to lay out the rows for your *Noodle Soup* quilt. Press the seam allowances of the rows as shown by the arrows. Rows 4, 6, 8, 10, 12, 14, and 16 are pressed the same way as row 2. Rows 5, 7, 9, 11, 13, and 15 are pressed the same as row 3.

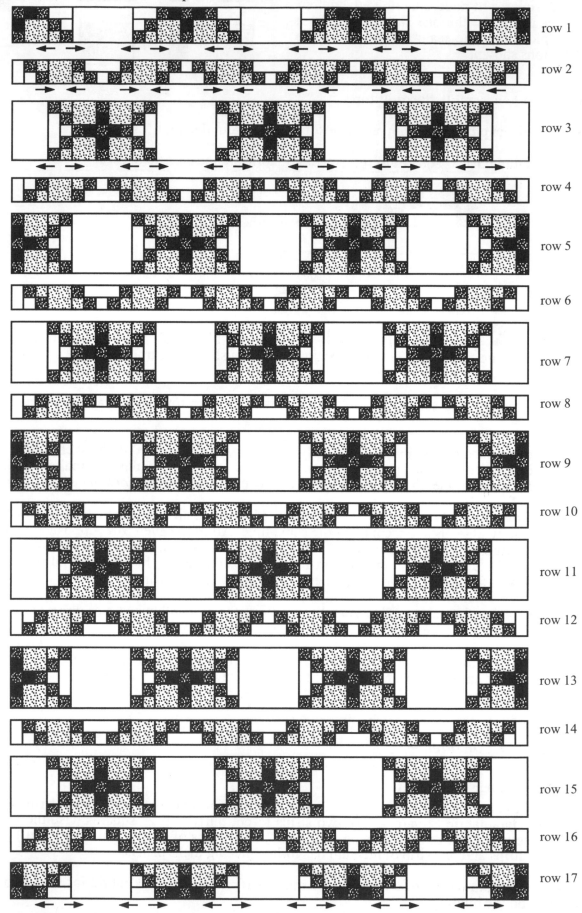

Pajama Party

The size of the quilt shown on page 27 is 46 1/2" x 61". Cutting the borders wider will make a generous lap size quilt. There is plenty of fabric allowed for this.

Fabric Requirements

This quilt was designed as a mystery pattern for a late night workshop. Simple rail blocks and nine patches make for a very quick quilt that is easy enough to piece during a pajama party with your quilting friends.

17 red noodles	
6 dark tan noodles	
6 dark green noodles	
Light cream	**1 yard**
Tan print	**5/8 yard**
Dark green border	**1 3/4 yards**
Binding	**3/4 yard**
Backing	**3 yards**

Cutting

Light cream

Cut thirteen strips 2" wide.

Tan print

Cut three strips 5" wide.
    Cut these strips into twenty 5" squares.

Dark green border

Cut a 25" wide x 1 3/4 yards long panel.
Reserve this for the borders.

From the remaining fabric
Cut seven 7 5/8" squares.
    Cut these squares twice, diagonally, to make four quarter-square triangles from each.
                    Yield: 28 triangles

Cut two 4 1/8" squares.
    Cut these squares once, diagonally, to make two half-square triangles from each.
                    Yield: 4 triangles

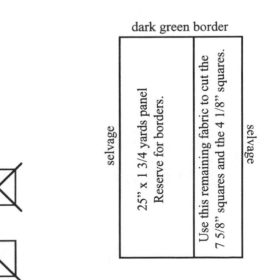

Piecing

Use six of the red strips, the six dark tan strips, and the six dark green strips to piece six A panels like the one shown below. Press the seam allowances away from the tan strips as shown by the arrows.

A - make 6 panels

Crosscut each of the six A panels into eight 5" wide sections.

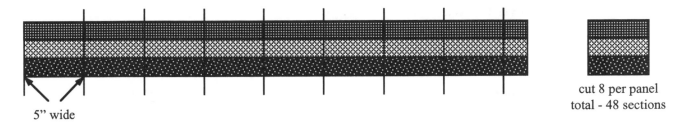

5" wide

cut 8 per panel
total - 48 sections

Use the remaining eleven red strips and the thirteen 2" wide cream strips to piece the panels shown below. Use the red strips randomly. Only one fill pattern is used to symbolize the reds to avoid confusion. Press all seam allowances toward the red strips.

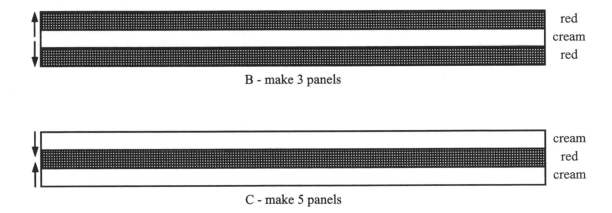

red
cream
red

B - make 3 panels

cream
red
cream

C - make 5 panels

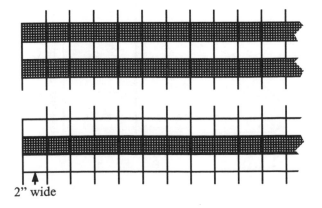

2" wide

Cross cut the B and C panels into sections that are 2" wide. Cut forty-three sections from the B's and eighty-six section from the C's.

Use these crosscut sections to make forty-three nine patch blocks. Press the seams toward the middle row.

make 43

38

The sketch below shows only one fill pattern to symbolize all of the reds, one for all of the dark tans, and one for all of the dark greens. See the photograph on page 27 for more specific fabric placement. You may choose to make a five fabric variation instead of the scrappy one. That is simple enough, just use one red, one dark tan, one dark green, one tan print, and one cream.

red   cream

dark tan   dark green

This quilt is set on point. It is pieced by sewing diagonal rows. Arrange all of the triangles, squares, rail blocks, and nine patch blocks to create the pattern as shown below. The four small dark green triangles are for the corners of the quilt. Be sure that you place each section in the correct position. **HINT:** The long side of the dark green in the rail block is always placed against a 5" square of tan print and never against a nine patch block.

Make the diagonal rows. See the exploded section below at the left to get started. Press all seam allowances away from the nine patches and away from the 5" squares of tan print.

Sew the rows together. Press the seams to one side.

Remove the selvage from your reserved border fabric. Cut four panels along the lengthwise grain (opposite direction from strip cutting). Cut these panels 3" wide for the version pictured on page 27 or up to 6" wide for a larger (56" x 69") finished size. Attach the borders with overlapped corners. See page 11 for more instruction on borders.

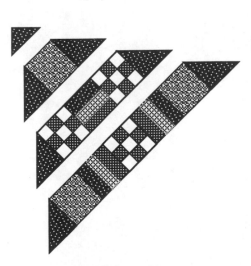

exploded view of the upper left corner of the quilt

Continue piecing diagonal rows.

Full or Queen Size

A full/queen size quilt would require fifteen A panels for making 120 rail blocks. Therefore, for the rail blocks you would need fifteen noodles of each of the three colors -- red, dark tan, and dark green.

A full/queen size would require 101 nine patch blocks. Use twenty red noodles and twenty-five cream noodles (1 3/4 yards) to make five B panels and ten C panels. Crosscut 101 2" wide sections from the B's and 202 2" wide sections from the C's.

A full/queen size would require forty-two 5" squares of tan print (1 yard), eleven 7 5/8" squares of dark green for the quarter-square triangles, and the same four corner triangles as the smaller size. Approximately 3 1/2 yards of dark green will be enough to cut the side triangles, corner triangles, and 10" wide borders. A second border 3" to 4" wide would make for a more generous fit on a queen size.

Full / Queen Size Layout

Doll Houses

The size of the quilt shown on page 18 is 43" x 43".

Fabric Requirements

Each of the nine houses requires a pair of noodles, one for the house and a second one for the roof and chimney. There will be enough left from these noodles to piece the border.

18 noodles	
White	**1 yard**
Binding	**1/2 yard**
Backing	**2 3/4 yards**

You may use less backing if you are creative in the way you piece the back.

Cutting

Noodles

Determine which nine strips are for the houses and which nine are for the roof/chimney sections.

From each of the nine house strips, cut
   one 2" x 8" rectangle,
   four 2" x 4" rectangles,
   three 2" x 3 1/2" rectangles, and
   one 2" square.

From each of the nine roof/chimney strips, cut
   one 2" x 8" rectangle,
   four 2" x 4" rectangles, and
   one 2" square.

White

Cut seven 2" wide strips.
   From these strips, cut
      two 2" x 27 1/2" rectangles,
      two 2" x 24 1/2" rectangles,
      nine 2" x 5" rectangles,
      nine 2" x 3 1/2" rectangles, and
      thirty-six 2" squares.

Cut three 1 1/4" wide strips
   From these strips, cut
      two 1 1/2" x 24 1/2" rectangles and
      six 1 1/4" x 8" rectangles.

Cut four 4" squares.

Piecing

Select one pair of "noodle" pieces to make a block (one group of house pieces and one group of roof/chimney pieces). Set aside the four 2" x 4" rectangles of both fabrics to be used for the border.

Place a 2" square of white on both ends of the 2" x 8" rectangle of *roof* fabric, right sides together. Stitch on the diagonal of both squares, in the directions shown by the dashed lines in the top sketch directly at the right. The finished roof section is shown in the second sketch. Check your work. If it is correct, trim away the excess, leaving 1/4" for seam allowances, as shown by the solid lines. Press the seam allowances toward the roof fabric.

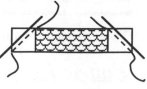

roof - make 1

Use one 2" x 5" rectangle of white, the 2" square of chimney fabric, and a 2" square of white to piece the top row of the block. Press the seam allowances toward the chimney.

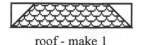

chimney - make 1

Use the three 2" x 3 1/2" rectangles of house fabric, the 2" square of house fabric, one 2" x 3 1/2" rectangle of white, and one 2" square of white to piece the door and window section of the house. First, sew the two squares together and press the seam allowances toward the house fabric. Sew the entire section together, as shown directly at the right, and press the seam allowances in the directions shown by the arrows.

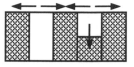

door and window
section - make 1

Arrange all of the rows from above with the remaining 2" x 8" rectangle of house fabric to complete the block. Sew the rows together and press the seam allowances in the directions shown by the arrows.

Repeat the above instructions to complete nine house blocks.

house block - make 9

Sew three rows of three houses, placing a 1 1/4" x 8" rectangle of white (sashing) between the house blocks. Press the seam allowances away from the houses.

Use a 1 1/4" x 24 1/2" rectangle as sashing between rows 1 and 2 and the second one as sashing between rows 2 and 3. Sew the rows and sashing together. Press all seam allowances toward the sashes.

Attach a 2" x 24 1/2" rectangle to the top of the quilt and the second one to the bottom. Press the seam allowances toward these rectangles.

Attach a 2" x 27 1/2" rectangle to each of the two sides of the quilt. Press the seam allowances toward these rectangles.

Arrange the 2" x 4" rectangles of house and roof fabrics in a pleasing order and make four pieced borders. Each border uses one rectangle of each fabric. Press the seam allowances to one side.

Attach a pieced border to both sides of the quilt. Press the seam allowances away from the pieced borders. Sew a 4" square of white to both ends of the remaining two borders. Press the seam allowances toward the squares. Attach these borders to the top and bottom edges of the quilt. Press the seam allowances away from the pieced borders.

Options to Consider --

Lap, Twin, Full, or Queen Size

In the sketch below, there are twenty house blocks set with 1 1/2" wide sashes (cut 2" wide) and the same pieced border as for the nine block quilt. A four inch wide outer border has been added. This quilt measures 52 1/2" x 61 1/2", a lap size. Consider the same setting for a bed size quilt. Make the outer border wider (8" - 10") on the bed size quilts. The suggested numbers of blocks for the bed size quilts are: thirty-five blocks for the twin (5 blocks x 7 rows), forty-two blocks for the full size (6 blocks x 7 rows), and fifty-six blocks for a queen size (7 blocks x 8 rows).

Banner

Consider using only three to five blocks to make one row, either vertical or horizontal. A vertical row would be attractive hanging on a narrow wall space next to the door in an entryway. A horizontal row would make a great quilt to hang above a fireplace mantel or a child's headboard.

March Winds

The size of the quilt shown on page 28 is 64" x 76".

Fabric Requirements

When selecting fabrics for *March Winds*, I chose to use three basic colors. The results are most effective if you keep the values close. For example, all of the blues are quite dark. On the other hand, vary the color a little so that it doesn't look as if you have used only one fabric. The blues in this quilt ranged from turquoise to blue violet, and the reds ranged from rusty orange-reds to violet reds.

Tans	**40 noodles**
Dark blues	**32 noodles**
Reds	**23 noodles**
Dark blue border	**2 1/4 yards**
Binding	**3/4 yard**
Backing	**4 yards**

Cutting

Label the pieces as suggested to keep them straight as you construct the quilt.

Tan noodles

From each of eighteen noodles, cut four 2" x 3 1/2" rectangles (72 rectangles, total). Label these A to be used for the pinwheel blades of the blocks with dark blue background.

Cut seven of the whole (42" long) noodles in half to make two pieces that are each approximately 2" x 21". Reserve thirteen of the fourteen pieces to be used for strip-piecing and label these B.

From the remainder (leftovers of the pinwheel blade strips, the fourteenth 2" x 21" piece from above, and the other fifteen noodles, cut
124 rectangles that are 2" x 6 1/2" (Label these C.) and
128 squares (2"). Label these squares D.

Dark blue noodles

From each of the thirty-two noodles, cut four 2" x 3 1/2" rectangles (128 rectangles, total). Label these E to be used for the pinwheel blades of the blocks with tan background.

Use the leftovers from above to cut
eight 2" x 21" rectangles (Label these F.),
seventy-two 2" x 6 1/2" rectangles (Label these G.), and
seventy-two 2" squares. Label these squares H.

Cutting, continued

Red noodles

Cut eleven of the noodles in half to make two pieces that are each approximately 2" x 21". Label (I) and reserve twenty-one of the twenty-two pieces to be used for strip-piecing.

Cut the remainder of the strips into 240 squares (2"). Label these squares J.

Dark blue border

Cut the 2 1/4 yards of border in half, lengthwise, making two panels that are approximately 21" x 2 1/4 yards.

Reserve one panel for the borders.

Cut the second panel into the following pieces:
twenty-two 2" x 6 1/2" rectangles (Label these K.) and
eighteen 2" x 3 1/2" rectangles (Label these L.).

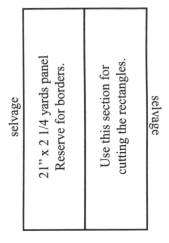

Piecing

Although the fabrics are used randomly in the quilt, to avoid confusion, only three fill patterns will be used to symbolize the many fabrics.

tan   red   dark blue

Use the B pieces and thirteen I pieces to make thirteen M panels like the one shown directly at the right. Press the seam allowances toward the red (I) pieces.

Panel M - make 13

Use the F pieces and remaining eight I pieces to make eight N panels. Press the seam allowances toward the red (I) pieces.

Panel N - make 8

Crosscut the M and N panels into sections that are 2" wide. Stack the panels, if desired, as described on page 9. Cut 128 sections from the M panels and seventy-two sections from the N panels.

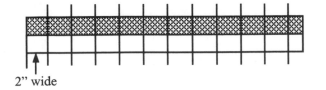

2" wide

M
cut 128

N
cut 72

Use the A pieces, H pieces, and the sew and flip technique to make seventy-two O units like the one at the right. *It is imperative that the completed units look exactly like the one shown. Do not make any reverses.* See below for more instruction on the sew and flip technique.

O - make 72

Sew and Flip Technique

Place a square on one end of each rectangle, right sides together.

Stitch on the diagonal, as shown by the dashed line in figure 1. Flip the corner up to check your work. *__It is imperative that the completed units look exactly like the sketch at the top of the page!__* If it is correct, trim the excess as shown by the solid line, leaving 1/4" for seam allowances. Press the seam allowances toward the small triangle.

fig. 1

Use the E pieces, D pieces, and the sew and flip technique to make 128 P units like the one at the right. *It is imperative that the completed units look exactly like the one shown. Do not make any reverses.*

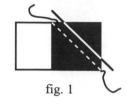

P - make 128

Use the O and P sections from above, 200 of the red 2" squares (J), and the sew and flip technique to complete the O and P units shown below. This time you will stitch the diagonal seam in the opposite direction. See figure 2.

completed O
make 72

completed P
make 128

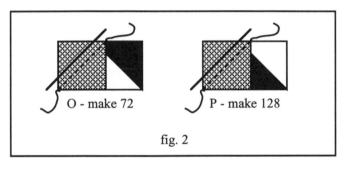

O - make 72

P - make 128

fig. 2

Sew the completed O units to the N sections from the previous page. Press the seam allowances in the direction shown by the arrow. Pay close attention to the positions of the pieces.

make 72

Use the seventy-two units you just completed to make eighteen pinwheel blocks. Use the four units that have the same pinwheel blade fabric to make a block. Make sure there is a red square in all four corners of the block. Press the seam allowances in the directions shown by the arrows.

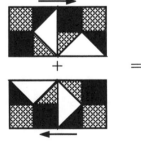

make 18

Sew the completed P units to the M sections from the previous page. Press the seam allowances in the direction shown by the arrow. Pay close attention to the positions of the pieces.

make 128

46

Use the 128 units you just completed to make thirty-two pinwheel blocks. Use the four units that have the same pinwheel blade fabric to make a block. Make sure there is a red square in all four corners of the block. Press the seam allowances in the directions shown by the arrows.

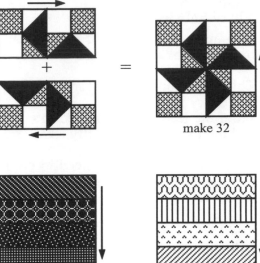

make 32

Use the 2" x 6 1/2" rectangles randomly to piece eighteen dark and thirty-one light rail blocks. Press the seam allowances to one side. Different fill patterns were used in the sketches of the rail blocks to show that each block uses four rectangles of different fabrics.

make 18   make 31

Sew a 2" square of red (J) to both ends of the eighteen L rectangles. Press the seam allowances toward the L's. These units are used alternately around the outside edges with the K pieces to create a border.

make 18

Arrange the pinwheel blocks, rail blocks, pieced border rectangles (from directly above), K rectangles, and the four remaining 2" squares of red (The four red squares are the corners of the quilt.) to make the quilt shown on page 28.

Sew the quilt together by piecing horizontal rows. Press the seam allowances away from the pinwheel blocks and toward the rail blocks. Press the seam allowances of the top and bottom rows toward the 2" x 6 1/2" rectangles.

Sew the rows together. Press the seam allowances to one side.

Remove the selvage from the reserved border fabric. Cut the fabric lengthwise (opposite from strip cutting) into four 4 1/2" wide panels. Use these to add borders with overlapped corners. See page 11 for more instruction on borders.

Options to Consider --

Twin Size

Due to the small scale of the pieces in this quilt, I have opted to give only a suggestion for a twin size quilt. I would recommend you select a different pattern with a larger scale for making a full or queen size.

To make a twin size you need only to widen the outer border. Purchase an additional yard of border fabric. Reserve 2 1/4 yards for an 8" - 10" wide border, and cut the remainder into the K and L rectangles.

Three Fabric Version

A simplified three fabric version can be made as shown below. This is a smaller quilt, which measures 45" x 57" when completed. Replace the rail blocks with 6 1/2" squares.

This quilt requires 1 3/4 yards of light, 2 yards of dark, and 1 1/8 yards of the accent (red) fabric.

From the light you will need to cut the following: seventeen 6 1/2" squares, four 2" strips for making the M sections, fifty-six 2" x 3 1/2" rectangles, and seventy-two 2" squares.

From the dark you will need to cut the following: fourteen 6 1/2" squares, three 2" strips for making the N sections, eighteen 2" x 6 1/2" rectangles, eighty-six 2" x 3 1/2" rectangles (fourteen for the border pieces and seventy-two for the pinwheels), and fifty-six 2" squares.

From the accent fabric you will need to cut the following: fifteen 2" wide strips. Use seven for strip piecing, and cut the other eight into 160 squares (2").

Make fourteen pinwheels with dark background and eighteen pinwheels with light background.

Complete the quilt as directed for the larger multiple fabric version.

Twice Broken Dishes

The size of the quilt shown on page 20 is 52" x 68".

Fabric Requirements

Years ago, before I had the idea of having ready-cut strips on hand for projects, I made the blocks of this quilt from the leftovers of a scrappy king size log cabin quilt I had made for my mother. In true 1980's fashion, there were a lot of country blue and rose colored strips, and I found that half of my blocks were bluish and half of them pinkish. Now, I should tell you, I never appreciated that period in home decorating. The last thing I had hoped to make was a pink and blue checkerboard quilt! So, before stashing the blocks with the other UFO's (Un-Finished Objects), I thought I'd give the blocks one last try by grouping similar colors and values. The result was fabulous. I was so pleased that I took the time to hand quilt this one.

FYI: Several of the fabrics have faded even though this quilt has never been exposed to sunlight. Please use the best fabrics you can find to make your quilts. Quilts only last as long as their weakest fabric.

Try selecting noodles that will create a movement in your quilt.

35 noodles	
Background	**4 1/4 yards**
Narrow inner border	**1/2 yard**
Binding	**3/4 - 1 yard**

The quilt on page 20 has a 3/4" wide binding to match the 3/4" narrow border. For this width, purchase 1 yard and cut the binding strips 4 3/4" wide. Attach them to the quilt using a 3/4" seam allowance. For a 1/2" wide binding purchase 3/4 yard. See page 13 for more information on bindings.

Backing	**3 1/4 yards**

Cutting

Background

Cut thirty-five strips 2" wide.

Narrow inner border

Cut eight strips 1 1/4" wide.

Piecing

Sew each of the noodles to a strip of background as shown below. Press the seam allowances toward the noodles.

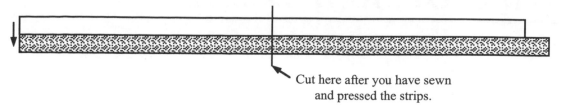

Cut here after you have sewn
and pressed the strips.

Cut each of the panels from above in half according to the shorter strip of the pair.

Place the two halves of the same panel together, right sides together. Position them so that the colors oppose each other. See the sketch directly at the right.

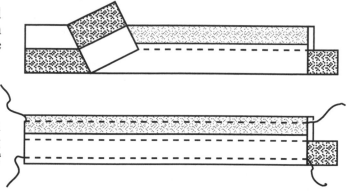

Sew the pairs from above into a tube. In other words, stitch along **both** of the long sides, as shown by the dashed lines. ***Do not turn the tube right side out.***

Make a template (page 15) and use double stick tape to fix it to the corner of a ruler.

HINT #1: The easiest way to make the template is as follows: Use your rotary cutter with an old blade to cut a 4 7/8" square of paper. Cut that square once on the diagonal to create two perfect templates.

4 7/8"
square

HINT #2: If you have a small Easy Angle Tool you can use it in place of the template. It is exactly the correct size and shape. Other triangle tools, such as the Omnigrid 96, can be used, as well. Lay any triangle tool you are considering over the template to see what markings to use.

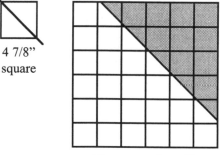

6" square ruler with
template taped to corner

Use the template or triangle tool from above to cut four sections from each of the tubes as shown below. Align the long side of the template with the edge of the tube. The sections may be slightly flat at the opposite corner. This is within the seam allowance and will not affect the result.

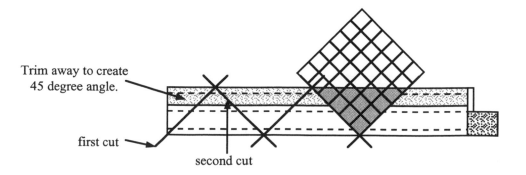

Trim away to create
45 degree angle.

first cut

second cut

Remove the few stitches at the corner of the sections, open the sections, and press the seam allowances toward the noodle fabric. Press carefully because the outer edges are on the bias.

Sew the sections into blocks like the one shown at the right. Use four sections of the same fabric to complete the block. Carefully press the seam allowances as shown by the arrows.

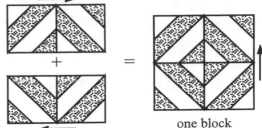

one block
make 35

Arrange the blocks into seven rows of five blocks. Refer to the photo on page 20. Sew the blocks into horizontal rows. Press the seam allowances of the odd rows to the left. Press the seam allowances of the even rows to the right.

Sew the rows together. Press the seam allowances to one side.

Remove the selvages and cut the remaining two yards of background fabric lengthwise (opposite from strip cutting) into four outer border panels. The borders in the quilt shown on page 20 are cut 6" wide. There is enough fabric to cut borders any width up to 10".

Attach the narrow inner border and the outer border with overlapped corners. Refer to page 11 for more instruction on borders.

Options to Consider --

Twin, Full, or Queen Size

It is simple to make this quilt any size you like. The finished size of the block is 8", so just calculate the number of blocks you need for the size desired. Each block uses one strip of background fabric and one noodle.

Suggested numbers of blocks for bed size quilts, assuming 8" - 10" wide outer borders, are the following:

Twin size   54 blocks (6 blocks x 9 rows)
Full size   72 blocks (8 blocks x 9 rows)
Queen size   90 blocks (9 blocks x 10 rows), or for a generous fit
                 110 blocks (10 blocks x 11 rows)

Scrappy Version

Use light and dark noodles and omit the control background fabric. Make sure you have enough contrast between the two strips in each block so that the pattern will show. If you choose to use some mediums, pair them with either a very light or a very dark strip to create contrast.

Contrast in color is another way to make sure you can see the pattern. A light pink strip paired with a medium to dark green will have more contrast than a light green strip paired with a medium to dark green.

Album Quilt - Block Assembly

The size of the quilt shown on page 25 is 62" x 74".

Fabric Requirements

Select your strips in sets of four. The four strips in each set will be used to make one Album block complete with the narrow accent border. Each set should contain one strip of each of the following: main print, primary accent, background, and secondary accent. If you choose, you may omit the accent border (secondary accent strip) and use a wider sashing. See the photograph on page 25 for some examples of fabric combinations.

80 noodles (twenty sets of four, see above for details)

Sashing & signature section (light cream) 3/4 yard
Buy 1 1/4 yards and cut the sashes 2" x 12 1/8" if you omit the secondary accent fabric.

Narrow inner border (dark green)	**5/8 yard**
Outer border (rust and green print)	**2 yards**
Cornerstones (rust)	**1/4 yard**
Binding	**3/4 yard**
Backing	**4 yards**

Cutting

Noodles

Label the pieces and keep the sets together to avoid confusion as you sew the blocks.

Main print strips -- From each of the twenty strips, cut
  two 2" x 8" rectangles (Label these A.),
  two 2" x 5" rectangles (Label these B.),
  two 2" x 3 1/2" rectangles (Label these C.), and
  two 2" squares (Label these D.).

Background strips -- From each of the twenty strips, cut
  four 2" squares (Label these E.).
  Reserve the remainder of each strip for strip-piecing.

Primary accent strips
  Reserve these for strip-piecing.

Secondary accent strips -- From each of the twenty strips, cut
  one 2" x 11 1/8" rectangle and
  one 2" x 12 1/8" rectangle.
  Split each of these rectangles lengthwise, making two 1" x 11 1/8" rectangles (Label these F.) and two 1" x 12 1/8" rectangles (Label these G.).

Sashing

Cut two strips 12 1/8" wide.
See the fabric requirements on the previous page prior to cutting these.
If you are using a secondary accent, cut these strips into forty-nine 1" x 12 1/8" rectangles.

Use the remainder of this fabric or three 2" wide strips of a different light fabric to cut the rectangles for the signature area of the block. From your fabric of choice, cut twenty (one per block) 2" x 5" rectangles (Label these H.).

Narrow inner border

Cut eight strips 2" wide.

Outer border

Remove the selvage and cut four lengthwise panels (opposite from strip cutting) that are 6" x 2 yards for the borders.

Cornerstones

Cut one strip 6" wide.
Cut this strip into four 6" squares.

Cut one strip 1" wide.
Cut this strip into thirty 1" squares.

Cut four 2" squares.

Piecing

Use one set of four fabrics to piece a block as follows:

Sew the remainder of the background strip to the primary accent strip, as shown at the right. Press the seam allowances toward the accent fabric.

Crosscut the panel from above into sixteen 2" wide sections.

Lay out the crosscut sections from above with the other pieces for the block, as shown in the exploded diagram directly at the right. Sew the pieces together to make the horizontal rows shown.

Press all of the seam allowances away from the main fabric.

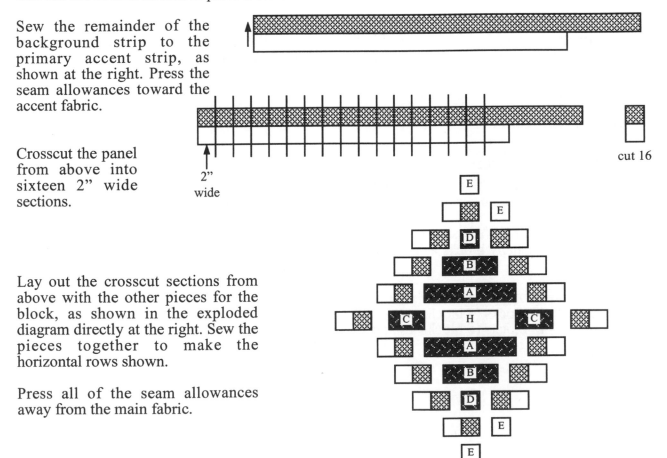

Sew the rows together and press the seam allowances away from the middle row.

Repeat to complete twenty blocks.

Use your rotary cutter and ruler to trim away the points around all four sides of the blocks, *leaving 1/4" beyond the corners of the primary accent fabric for seam allowances.*

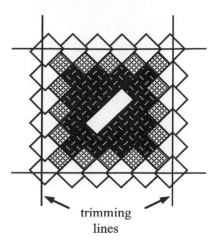

trimming
lines

Frame the blocks with pieces F and G, the secondary accent fabrics.

Arrange the blocks with the sashes and cornerstones into five rows of four blocks. Refer to the photo on page 25. Assemble the quilt by sewing horizontal rows. Press the seam allowances toward the sashes in all rows.

Sew the rows together. Press the seam allowances toward the sashing rows.

Measure and determine the average length and width of the quilt top. Piece two narrow inner borders to fit the length of the quilt. Attach these to the sides of the quilt. Press the seam allowances toward the borders.

Piece two narrow inner borders to fit the width of the quilt. Sew a 2" square cornerstone to both ends of these two borders. Press the seam allowances away from the squares. Attach the borders to the top and bottom of the quilt.

Measure and determine the length and width of the quilt now that the inner border pieces have been added. Trim two of the outer border pieces to the average length of the quilt. Trim the other two outer border pieces to the average width of the quilt.

Attach the side borders. Press the seam allowances toward the borders. Sew a 6" square cornerstone to both ends of the top and bottom borders. Press the seam allowances toward the borders. Attach these borders. Press the seam allowances toward the borders.

Options to Consider --

Twin, Full, or Queen Size

The finished size of the block before adding the secondary accent frame is 10 5/8". The finished size of the block with the secondary accent frame added is 11 5/8".

Enlarging this quilt is very simple. As you have discovered, each block requires three or four noodles. Make as many blocks as needed for your desired size. Use wider (8" - 10") borders for bed size quilts.

Twin size   24 blocks (4 blocks x 6 rows)
Full size   30 blocks (5 blocks x 6 rows)
Queen size   42 blocks (6 blocks x 7 rows)

Album Quilt - Row Assembly

The size of the quilt shown on page 24 is 57 1/2" x 68".

Fabric Requirements

Fabric selection for this quilt was simple. I gathered a rainbow of fabrics from the Benartex collection of Fossil Ferns. Anything that contrasts with the background will work well for you. Choose a strong control fabric for the chains between the album "blocks".

20 noodles (for the "blocks")	
Background (cream)	**2 1/4 yards**
Signature sections (muslin)	**1/4 yard**
Chains & outer border (blue-gray)	**3 yards**
Binding	**3/4 yard**
Backing	**3 3/4 yards**

Cutting

Noodles

Label the pieces and keep the sets together to avoid confusion as you assemble the quilt.

From each of the twenty strips, cut the following:
two 2" x 8" rectangles (Label these A.),
two 2" x 5" rectangles (Label these B.),
two 2" x 3 1/2" rectangles (Label these C.),
and two 2" squares (Label these D.).
Keep the small leftover tails from the noodles handy for use during piecing the quilt top.

Background

Cut twenty-eight strips 2" wide.
Reserve twenty-two for strip-piecing.

Cut two 2" squares from the end of one strip. These are used in the upper left and lower right corners of the quilt. The remainder of this strip and the other five are used for the narrow inner border of the quilt.

Muslin

Cut three strips 2" wide.
Cut these strips into twenty 2" x 5" rectangles. (Label these E.).

Chains

Cut twelve strips 2" wide.

Remove the selvages from a two yard piece of the remaining fabric. Cut four panels lengthwise (opposite from strip cutting) 6" wide x 2 yards long for the outer borders.

Piecing

Use twenty-two 2" strips of background and twelve 2" strips of chain fabric to piece the panels shown below. Press all seam allowances toward the chain fabric.

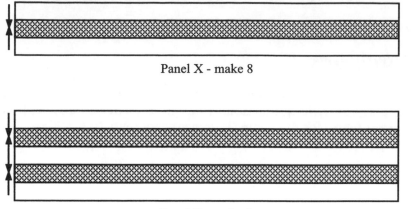

Panel X - make 8

Panel Y - make 2

Crosscut the X and Y panels into sections that are 2" wide.

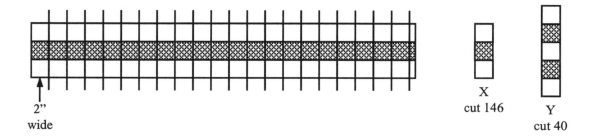

2"
wide

X
cut 146

Y
cut 40

Assembling the Quilt Top --

This quilt is assembled by piecing diagonal rows, not blocks.

HINT #1: Here is an easy way to determine where each of the twenty fabrics will be placed in the quilt. Use the leftover tails and arrange them in a pleasing order, placing four pieces in a row and making five rows. It is much easier to move these small pieces around on a table top until you are happy, as opposed to laying out the entire quilt and moving many pieces. When you are pleased with their arrangement, tape or staple the tails, in position, to a piece of paper. This becomes your reference key to positioning the fabrics.

HINT #2: Lay out only a few rows of the quilt at one time. Sew them together and lay out the next few rows. In other words, eat the elephant one bite at a time. There are so many pieces that even with a large stationary design wall it will get confusing.

HINT #3: Photocopy and enlarge the layout shown on the following page. Mark or mask off the rows, or fold them under, as you piece them. Look only at the row you are piecing to avoid confusion.

HINT #4: The Y sections are marked in the layout on the next page. The X sections are used everywhere else that you need a chain section, but they are not marked. The diagram would be too busy to read. The "block" pieces are labeled in an enlarged view at the top of the next page. After a few rows you will begin to see the pattern.

Place the rectangles of the "block" fabrics in the order shown in the enlarged section at the right.

Piece the quilt top by making diagonal rows, beginning in the upper left corner as shown by the exploded section of the quilt.

When constructing the rows, all seam allowances are pressed toward the "block" fabrics.

Sew the rows together. Press all of the seam allowances away from the center row of the quilt.

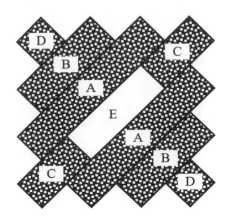

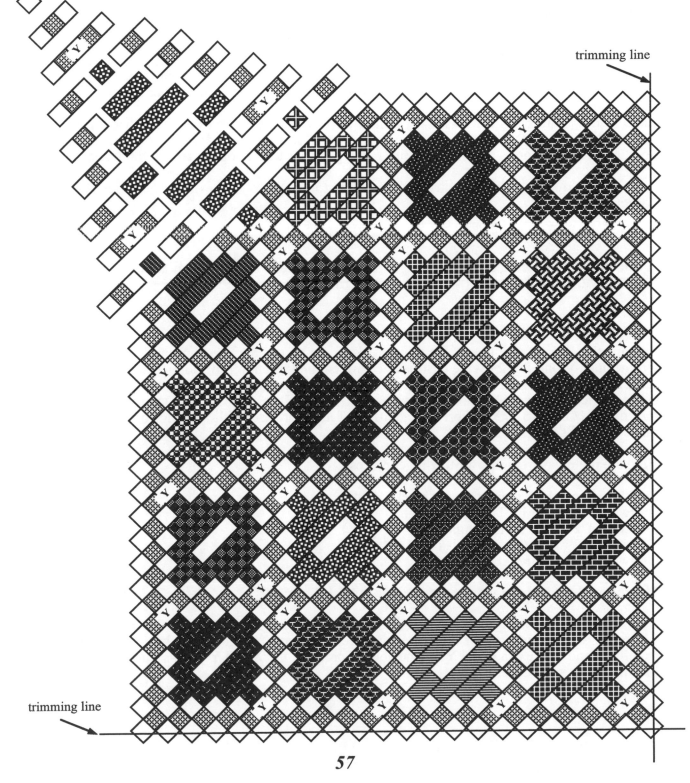

trimming line

trimming line

Use your rotary cutter and ruler to trim away the points around all four sides of the quilt, *leaving 1/4" beyond the corners of the chain pieces for seam allowances*, as shown by the lines along the right and bottom edges of the quilt in the diagram on the previous page.

Use the reserved 2" strips of background fabric to make a narrow inner border. Attach the border with overlapped corners. Press the seam allowances toward the border. See page 11 for more instruction on borders.

Attach the outer border with overlapped corners. Press the seam allowances toward the border.

Options to Consider --

Larger Quilt

It may be very confusing to make a full size quilt or larger using this pattern. I suggest you consider using the block assembly in the previous pattern on page 52 for larger quilts.

Larger quilts using this row assembly will require two to three times as much background and chain fabric in order to make many more X and Y sections. In addition you will need more noodles. Here are some suggested layouts for larger sizes to get you started, if you insist:

A twin size quilt would use thirty-five noodles (5 blocks x 7 rows), and a wider (8" - 10") border.

A full size quilt would use forty-two noodles (6 blocks x 7 rows), and a wider (8" - 10") border.

A queen size quilt would use forty-eight noodles (6 blocks x 8 rows), an additional border (4" finished width), and a wider (8" x 10") outer border.

Larger Quilt Made With Larger Pieces

Perhaps the easiest way to enlarge this quilt is to cut all of your pieces from 2 1/2" wide strips. Unfortunately one 2 1/2" wide strip is not long enough to cut all of the pieces needed for each "block". You will need a second one. Again, you will need more of both the background and chain fabrics. A twenty "block" quilt with these larger pieces will have an approximate finished size of 59 1/2" x 73 1/2" before the addition of any borders. With a border or two, you could make this quilt fit a full size bed.

Here are the measurements for the larger pieces:

From the two 2 1/2" strips for the "blocks", cut
    two 2 1/2" x 10 1/2" rectangles (A),
    two 2 1/2" x 6 1/2" rectangles (B),
    two 2 1/2" x 4 1/2" rectangles (C), and
    two 2 1/2" squares (D).

The rectangles for the signature area (E) are cut 2 1/2" x 6 1/2".

Your other strips (background and chain fabrics) will need to be cut 2 1/2" wide, as well, and you will need many more of them. For the twenty "block" version, start by making two extra panel X's and one extra panel Y. Remember to crosscut the X and Y panels into 2 1/2" sections for this larger size, not 2"!

Liberty Stars

The size of the quilt shown on page 26 is 45" x 55 1/2".

Fabric Requirements

I didn't have a good selection of light fabrics in my homespun collection, so I chose to use a single background fabric. This quilt would be very successful if you used one strip of twelve different background fabrics.

12 dark blue or green noodles (for the stars)

7 red noodles (for the primary chain)

6 dark tan/gold noodles (for the secondary chain)

Background (light)	**7/8 yard**
Sashing (dark green)	**3/4 yard**
Border	**1 1/2 yards**
Binding	**3/4 yard**
Backing	**3 yards**

Cutting

Dark blue or green noodles

Each block will use eight quarter-square triangles to make the star. Use the template on page 16 or an Omnigrid 98 triangle tool to cut eight 3" (finished size) quarter-square triangles from each of the twelve strips. *See pages 64 and 65 for more instruction on cutting these pieces.*

Red noodles

Cut twelve 2" squares from each of six noodles. These squares are for piecing the blocks.

Cut twenty 2" squares from the seventh noodle. These squares are the cornerstones.

Dark tan/gold noodles

Cut twelve 2" squares from each of the six noodles.

Background*

Cut eleven strips 2" wide.
> Use six of these strips to cut ninety-six 3" (finished size) quarter-square triangles. *See pages 64 and 65 for more instruction on cutting these pieces.*

> Use five of these strips to cut ninety-six 2" squares.

*If you use one strip of twelve different fabrics, cut eight triangles and eight squares from each strip.

Cutting, continued

Sashing

Cut two strips 9 1/2" wide.
Cut these strips into thirty-one 2" x 9 1/2" rectangles.

Border

Trim the selvages from the border fabric. Split it lengthwise (opposite from strip cutting) into four panels that are 6 1/2" wide x 1 1/2 yards long.

Piecing

Get organized before you begin to sew. Make twelve groups of pieces, one group for each block. Each group will contain four different fabrics and the following pieces:

 eight dark blue or green quarter-square triangles of one fabric,

six red 2" squares of one red fabric,

 six tan/gold 2" squares of one tan/gold fabric, and

eight quarter-square triangles and eight 2"squares of one background fabric.

Select one group of fabrics to piece a block as directed below.

Use all of the squares in the group to piece four patch blocks like those shown below. Press the seam allowances in the directions shown by the arrows.

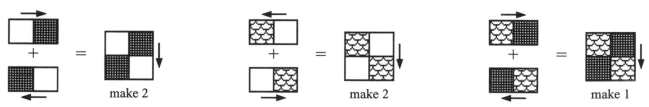

make 2   make 2   make 1

Use the eight dark and eight light quarter-square triangles to make four hourglass units. Sew the triangles into pairs. Press the seam allowances toward the dark. Sew the pairs together and press to one side. Trim the dog ears.

make 4

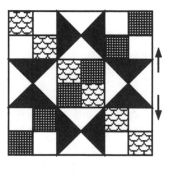

Arrange the four patches and hourglass units to make a star block. Piece the block by sewing horizontal rows. Press the seam allowances away from the hourglass units. Sew the rows together. Press the seam allowances away from the middle row.

Repeat the above steps to complete twelve star blocks.

Arrange the quilt three blocks wide and four rows long. Place the 2" x 9 1/2" green sashes between the blocks and along the outer edges. Put the red cornerstones into position.

Complete the quilt top by making horizontal rows. Press the seam allowances toward the sashes in all rows. Sew the rows together. Press the seam allowances toward the sashing rows.

Attach the border, using overlapped corners. Press the seam allowances toward the border. See page 11 for more instruction on borders.

Options to Consider --

Twin, Full, or Queen Size

This is another simple quilt to enlarge. The blocks are 9", finished size. Determine how many blocks you need for the size quilt you desire. Here is help to figure the number of noodles you need:

One 2" strip of background will make enough pieces for one block.
One 2" strip of star fabric will make enough triangles for two blocks.
One 2" strip of red chain will make enough squares for three blocks.
One 2" strip of dark tan/gold will make enough squares for three blocks.

With the same setting as directed above (sashing and cornerstones) and a wider border (8" - 10"), the bed sizes will require:

Twin size   35 blocks (5 blocks x 7 rows)
Full size   42 blocks (6 blocks x 7 rows)
Queen size   56 blocks (7 blocks x 8 rows)

Alternate Setting Options

Try omitting the sashing and setting the star blocks alternately with chain blocks like the one shown at the right.

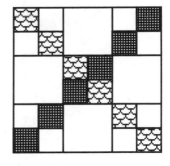

These blocks use the same four patch units as the star blocks, but the four hourglass units are replaced with four 3 1/2" squares of background fabric.

Sew the four patches and squares into horizontal rows. Press the seam allowances away from the four patches. Sew the rows together to complete the chain block. Press the seam allowances toward the middle row.

Using these alternate blocks makes a very attractive quilt whether the blocks are set squarely or on point. See the diagrams on the next page.

At left:

Twelve Liberty Stars set squarely with thirteen chain blocks

Below:

Twelve Liberty Star blocks set on point with six chain blocks

Lost Ships

The size of the quilt shown on page 22 is 62" x 79".

Fabric Requirements

This block looks much more difficult than it really is. Even more, it is as versatile as a Log Cabin block when it comes to setting options. With the block's strong diagonal line, it is possible to set it in Barn Raising, Fields and Furrows, etc. Try arranging your blocks in various settings to see what secondary patterns emerge.

48 noodles (for the ships)

Background (light)	**2 1/2 yards**
Border	**2 1/2 yards**

This measurement is for mitered corners. Overlapped corners require 2 1/8 yards.

Binding	**3/4 yard**
Backing	**4 3/4 yards**

Cutting

As you can see from the photograph on page 22, each block is constructed with pieces from one noodle and the background.

Noodles

Use the Omnigrid 98L triangle tool or the templates on page 16 to cut these pieces. See the following page for more instruction before cutting these pieces.

Cut the following from each 2" strip:
  one 12" (finished size) trapezoid,
  one 9" (finished size) trapezoid,
  one 6" (finished size) trapezoid, and
  one 3" (finished size) quarter-square triangle.

Background

Cut five strips 7 1/4" wide.
  Cut these strips into twenty-four 7 1/4" squares.
    Cut each square once, diagonally, to make two half-square triangles from each.
    Yield: 48 triangles

Cut twelve strips 3" wide.
  Cut these strips into 168 squares (3").
    Cut each square once, diagonally, to make two half-square triangles from each.
    Yield: 336 triangles

Cutting Trapezoids and Quarter-Square Triangles

Trapezoids and quarter-square triangles are easily cut from the noodles using an Omnigrid 98L triangle tool. Other tools, such as the Companion Angle, may work, too. Seam allowances have been built into the Omnigrid tool, so you will focus on the finished size. With the Omnigrid 98L, use the line directly below the number. Other tools are designed differently. Lay any tool that you are considering on the templates (page 16) to see exactly where they align.

A trapezoid is merely a four-sided shape that has two parallel sides and two sides that are not parallel. To cut a trapezoid that finishes to 12" long on the base (the longest of the four sides), align the Omnigrid 98L so that the bottom of the tool is along the bottom edge of the strip. This the longest piece you can cut with the Omnigrid 98L. Cut along both edges of the tool as shown in photo 4.

To cut the next piece, a 9" finished size trapezoid, rotate (Spin, don't flip it over.) the triangle a half turn (180 degrees). Place the 9" line along the top edge of the strip, and the side of the tool even with the angled edge of the strip. Cut. See photo 5.

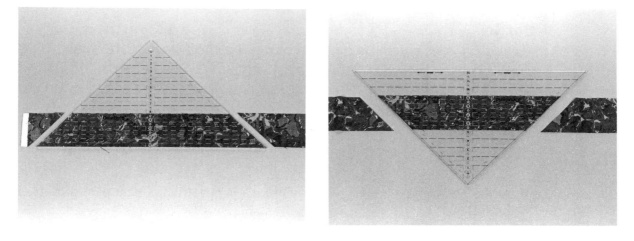

photo 4   photo 5

Rotate the Omnigrid 98L 180 degrees again, and align the 6" line on the bottom edge of the strip. Cut the 6" trapezoid. Rotate the Omnigrid 98L one last time, and align the 3" line with the top edge of the strip. Cut the 3" quarter-square triangle. This triangle will have a slightly flattened tip as shown in the template on page 16.

NOTE: Quarter-square triangles are usually cut by slicing a larger square twice, diagonally, into quarters to make four triangles from each square. To cut a triangle which measures 3", finished size, on the long edge of the triangle, the traditional rotary cutting method would require a 4 1/4" square. The method described in the paragraph above allows you to work with just your noodles and avoid cutting odd holes into yardage for the 4 1/4" squares.

If you do not have access to an Omnigrid 98L triangle, use double stick tape to position the four templates from page 16 onto another rotary cutting ruler. I find that a square which is at least 9 1/2" will allow you to put all four templates on it at one time. This simplifies things when you need to cut all four different sizes from your strips for the Lost Ships quilt. See photos 6 and 7 on the next page.

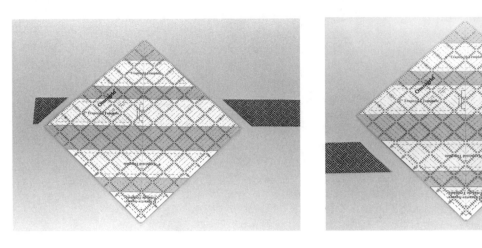

photo 6   photo 7

Piecing

The following instructions are for making one block.

Use only one ship fabric (noodle) per block.

Sew a small triangle of background to the 3" quarter-square triangle of ship fabric, making a half-square triangle unit. Press the seam allowances toward the ship fabric. Press carefully to avoid distorting the bias edges.

Sew a small triangle of background fabric to the side of the unit from above. Press the seam allowances in the direction shown by the arrow. Trim the dog ear.

Sew another small triangle to the adjacent side of the unit from above. Press the seam allowances in the direction shown by the arrow. Trim the dog ear.

Sew the largest trapezoid to a large triangle of background fabric. Press the seam allowances in the direction shown by the arrow.

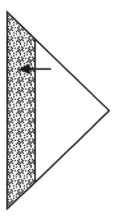

Sew a small triangle of background fabric to both ends of the two remaining trapezoids as shown directly below. Press the seam allowances as shown by the arrows. Trim the dog ears.

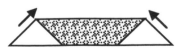
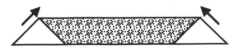

65

Sew the rows and sections together to complete the block shown at the right. Press the seam allowances in the directions shown by the arrows.

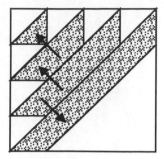

Lost Ship block
make 48

Repeat the above steps to make a total of forty-eight blocks.

Arrange the blocks into eight rows of six blocks. Place the blocks all in the same direction as in the quilt on page 22, or rotate them to create another pattern.

Sew the blocks into horizontal rows. Press the seam allowances of the odd rows to the left. Press the seam allowances of the even rows to the right. Sew the rows together. Press the seam allowances to one side.

Attach the border using mitered or overlapped corners. See page 11 for more instruction on borders.

Options to Consider --

Twin, Full, or Queen Size

This is another simple quilt to enlarge. The blocks are 8 1/2", finished size. Determine how many blocks you need for the size quilt you desire.

As you have seen, each block requires one noodle. More background fabric is needed for larger sizes, of course. I suggest about 3 yards for the twin, 4 yards for the full size, and 5 yards for the queen size. These allowances may be a bit generous, but they are good estimates. For wide borders with mitered corners you need the following amounts: twin size 2 3/4 yards; full size 2 3/4 yards; and queen size 3 yards.

With the addition of a second or wider border (8" - 10"), the bed sizes will require:

Twin size   54 blocks (6 blocks x 9 rows)*
Full size   63 blocks (7 blocks x 9 rows)*
Queen size   80 blocks (8 blocks x 10 rows)

*An odd number of rows will eliminate some of the setting possibilities. For example, Barn Raising requires an even number of blocks and rows to center the diamond on the quilt.

Pieced Accent Border

There is a good bit of each strip left after cutting the trapezoids and triangles for the blocks. Consider using these in a pieced border to accent your quilt.

Kaleidoscope

The size of the quilt shown on page 23 is 58" x 58".

Fabric Requirements

Entire books are available on Kaleidoscope quilts. Amazing secondary patterns, such as stars and circles, can be created by variations in fabric and value placement. I chose to use a collection of Hoffman fabrics to make this garden effect. Study other books and magazines to get more ideas for your Kaleidoscope quilt.

30 noodles, or more for variety	
Background (lt. blue batik)	**1 1/4 yards**
Border & accent triangles (lt. blue print)	**2 1/4 yards**
Binding	**3/4 yard**
Backing	**3 3/4 yards**

Cutting

Noodles

To get more variety in your blocks, cut the noodles in half, making two half-strips that are approximately 2" x 21" from each.

Background

Cut four strips 5" wide.
    These will be cut into wedges as described on the next page.

Cut three strips 3 1/2" wide.
    Cut these strips into twenty-six 3 1/2" squares.
        Cut each square once, diagonally, to make two half-square triangles from each.
                Yield: 52 triangles

Border & accent triangles

Cut a 15" x 2 1/4 yards panel, lengthwise, and reserve this for borders.

From the remainder of your border fabric, cut
        eight 5" x 18 1/2" rectangles,
        four 5" x 9 1/2" rectangles,
        four 5" squares, and
        twenty-four 3 1/2" squares.
            Cut each 3 1/2" square once, diagonally, to make two half-square triangles
            from each.   Yield: 48 triangles

Piecing

Select three of your half-strips to make a panel. Sew them together, off-setting them 3/4", as shown by the small trimmed section on the left in photo 8. Staggering the ends like this will make efficient use of your fabrics. Press the seam allowances to one side. Continue making panels until you have a total of twenty panels.

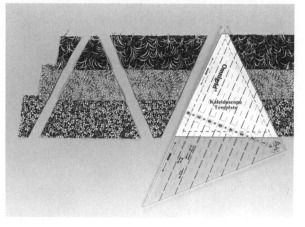

Use the template from page 15 or one of several kaleidoscope tools available for rotary cutting to cut the panels into wedges.

HINT: Use double stick tape to attach the template to any 45 degree triangle, as shown in the picture.

Cut eight wedges from each panel. You will notice that each panel yields four wedges with one fabric at the tip, and another four with that fabric at the base. Keep them in sets of four that are exactly alike.

Use the template to cut fifty-six wedges from the four 5" strips of background.

photo 8

Making the Blocks

It may help to read this entire section before beginning to piece the blocks.

Three different blocks are used to make the pattern in this quilt. Block A is made with two sets of pieced wedges, eight total. Block B is made with four pieced wedges and four background wedges. Block C is made with three pieced wedges and five background wedges.

NOTE: The B and C blocks use pieced wedges from different panels. After completing the A blocks, you will need to lay out the rest of the quilt top to determine where each of the remaining wedges should be placed. Refer to the photo on page 23 and the diagram on the next page for more guidance. You may choose to design the entire quilt before piecing any of the blocks. I laid out the whole quilt and decided to omit some of my wedges and replace them with others that I then made to get exactly what I wanted to complete the quilt.

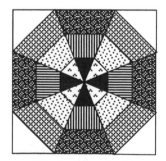

Block A - make 13

Block B - make 4
These blocks are used on the four sides of the center A block.

Block C - make 8
Use these blocks along the outer edges of the quilt.

To make the A blocks, sew the wedges into four pairs that are exactly alike. Press the seam allowances to one side, the same direction in all pairs.

Sew two pairs together to make half of the block. Match the seam lines carefully at the points of the wedges. Repeat to make the second half. Press the seam allowances to one side, in the same direction as the seam allowances in the first half were pressed. Sew the two halves together, making sure to match the seams and points at the center. Press the seam allowances to one side.

Attach the half-square triangles of background fabric to the four corners of each A block. Press the seam allowances toward the triangles. Trim the dog ears.

Lay out the A blocks as shown below. Use a group of four pieced wedges to complete the first starburst, as shown in the upper left corner. *Do not sew them onto the A block at this time.* Continue laying out the pieced wedges to complete each starburst until all of the pieced wedges are in place. There will be one set of four pieced wedges left over. These wedges are not needed for the quilt.

Fill in the B and C blocks with the wedges of background fabric. Construct these blocks in the same way that you made the A blocks. Use the half-square triangles of border/accent fabric to complete the corners. Trim the dog ears.

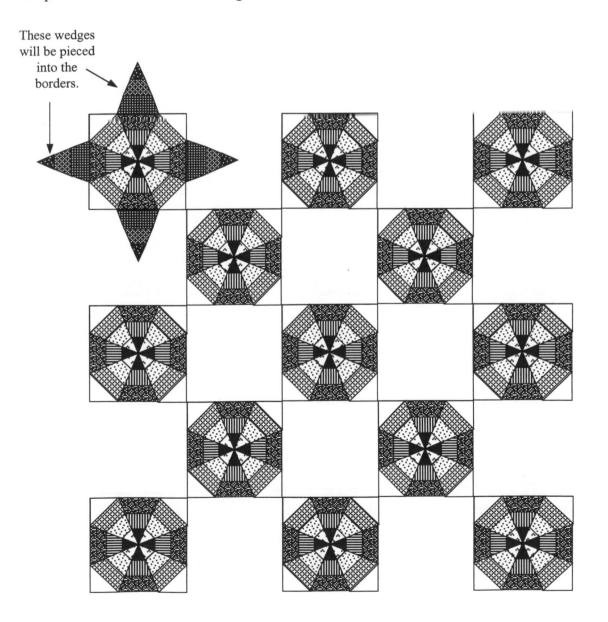

These wedges will be pieced into the borders.

Assembling the Quilt

Sew the twenty-five blocks together by making five horizontal rows of five blocks. Press the seam allowances away from the A blocks in all rows. Sew the rows together. Press the seam allowances to one side.

Use the trim-away template from page 15 to trim all of the rectangles and squares of border fabric, as directed below.

NOTE: Both ends of all of the 5" x 18 1/2" rectangles will be trimmed as shown in figure 1, but only one end of the 5" x 9 1/2" and one corner of the 5" squares will be trimmed (figures 2 and 3). *It is important that you trim two of these pieces as reverses. To do so, stack two of the same pieces, wrong sides together, and trim both at the same time. This will automatically make the reverses.*

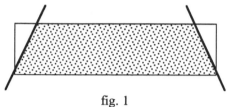 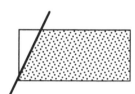

fig. 1	fig. 2	fig. 3
Trim both ends of the eight 5" x 18 1/2" rectangles.	Trim one end of the four 5" x 9 1/2" rectangles, being sure to make two reverses as directed above.	Trim one corner of the four 5" squares, being sure to make two reverses as directed above.

Use the trimmed pieces from above and the remaining pieced wedges to make the four borders shown below, making sure each specific pieced wedge is where it belongs to complete your design. Press the seam allowances away from the pieced wedges, as shown by the arrows.

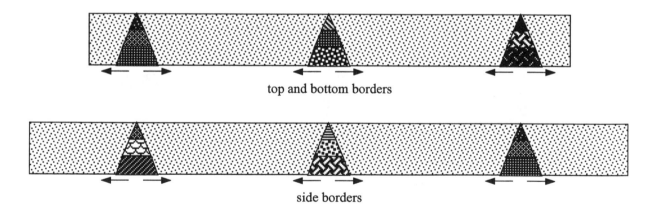

top and bottom borders

side borders

Attach the pieced top and bottom borders to the quilt, matching the seams and pinning as needed. Press the seam allowances toward the borders. Attach the pieced side borders. Press.

Remove the selvage from the reserved border panel. Split it lengthwise into four panels that are 3 1/2" x 2 1/4 yards long. Use these to add borders with overlapped corners. See page 11 for more instruction on borders.

Options to Consider --

Twin, Full, or Queen Size

This quilt is another that is simple to enlarge. The blocks are 9", finished size. Determine how many blocks you need for the size quilt you desire. The size of the quilt and the overall pattern will determine how many A, B, and/or C blocks you need.

With the addition of a second or wider border (8" - 10"), the bed sizes will require the following:

Twin size   54 blocks (6 blocks x 9 rows)*
Full size   63 blocks (7 blocks x 9 rows)
Queen size   80 blocks (8 blocks x 10 rows)*

*An odd number of blocks per row and an odd number of rows are necessary to achieve a symmetrical quilt when using the design that I used. The option below works with any number of blocks or rows.

Another Effect

Here is another look to the Kaleidoscope quilt. This quilt uses only A blocks. It is shown with few fabrics, but I suggest using many lights and darks. Notice the corner triangles. The difference is that two dark fabrics close in value were used instead of light as in the previous version. A quilt with thirty blocks measures 45" x 54" before adding any borders. It is a good lap size. As I mentioned in the Fabric Requirements section at the beginning of the pattern, many books and magazine articles feature Kaleidoscope quilts. Visit your local quilt shop and look for other options there.

Florida Quilt

The size of the quilt shown on page 21 is 55 1/2" x 71".

Fabric Requirements

Florida is one of the traditional names given to this quilt pattern. I'm not sure if this block was named for the state of Florida or if it came by that name in another way. The word *florida* can mean *flowered* or *covered with flowers* in Spanish. I think my quilt looks as if it has yellow blossoms peeking out from a white garden lattice. With changes in the placements of fabrics, this same quilt pattern has other traditional names, such as New Hampshire, Star Rays, Diamond String, and Oriental Splendor.

26 white noodles	
8 yellow noodles	
Blue background and border	**3 yards**
Binding	**3/4 yard**
Backing	**3 1/2 yards**

Cutting

White noodles

Cut these strips into 60 degree trapezoids using the template on page 15, a large Clearview Triangle tool, or a Super 60 tool. These trapezoids are different than the ones used in the *Lost Ships* quilt. Be sure you are using the correct template. ***See the next page for more details on cutting these trapezoids before beginning.***

Total: 126 trapezoids

cut 126

Yellow noodles

Cut these strips into 60 degree diamonds using the template on page 14 or with a rotary cutter and ruler. ***See the next page for more details on cutting these diamonds before beginning.***

Total: 126 diamonds

cut 126

Background

Cut five strips 6 1/2" wide.
> Cut these strips into forty-two large 60 degree triangles using the triangle template on page 14, a large Clearview Triangle tool, or a Super 60 tool. ***See the next page for more details on cutting these triangles before beginning.***

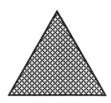

cut 42

Cutting, continued

Background

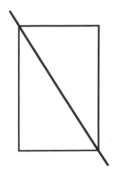

Cut one strip 11 1/2" wide.

Cut this strip into six 6 5/8" x 11 1/2" rectangles.

With the rectangles layered so that three of them are right side up and three of them are wrong side up, slice the rectangles once on the diagonal as shown in the sketch at the right. It is important that half of the rectangles are right side up and the second half is wrong side up to create the necessary reverse triangles. These are the side triangles for the ends of the rows.

Yield: 12 triangles, six of them reverses of the other six

Cutting the Trapezoids from the White Noodles

Use the template on page 15, a large 60 degree Clearview Triangle, or a Clearview Super 60 Tool to cut the trapezoids. If you are using one of the Clearview triangle tools, position it so that the strip is between the 6" and 8" lines of the tool. See photo 9 below. Rotate the tool or template and continue cutting trapezoids in the same manor, as described on page 64 in the Lost Ships pattern, until you have cut 126 trapezoids.

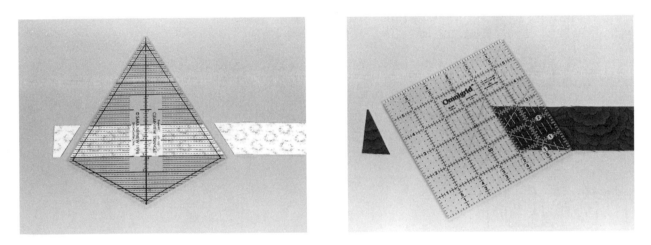

photo 9   photo 10

Cutting the Diamonds from the Yellow Noodles

Use the diamond template on page 14 to cut the diamonds, or rotary cut them as follows.

Align a 60 degree triangle tool or the 60 degree line on your rotary cutting ruler with the long edge of the strips and trim the ends, creating a 60 degree angle. Place the 2" line of your ruler along the newly trimmed edge as shown in photo 10. Cut along the edge of the ruler. Continue cutting diamonds in this way until you have cut 126 diamonds.

Cutting the Triangles from the 6 1/2" Strips of Background

Use the triangle template on page 14, a large 60 degree Clearview Triangle, or a Clearview Super 60 tool to cut these triangles. If you are using one of the triangle tools, position it so that the 6 1/2" line is on one edge of the strip and the tip of the triangle is on the opposite edge. See photo 11 on the next page. Continue rotating the triangle tool or template and cutting triangles until you have cut forty-two large triangles.

Piecing

Sew a trapezoid to the bottom of each large triangle of background (figure 1). Press the seam allowances toward the trapezoids.

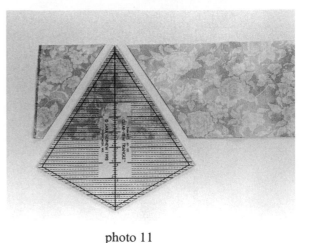

photo 11

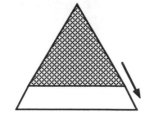

fig. 1
make 42

Sew a diamond to one end of forty-two trapezoids (figure 2). Press the seam allowances toward the trapezoids.

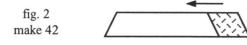

fig. 2
make 42

Sew the sections from figure 1 to those from figure 2. Press the seam allowances away from the large triangle. See figure 3.

Sew a diamond to both ends of the remaining forty-two trapezoids (figure 4). Press the seam allowances toward the trapezoids. Attach these sections to complete the blocks. Press the seam allowances away from the large triangle. See figure 5.

fig. 3
make 42

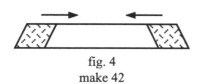

fig. 4
make 42

fig. 5
make 42 blocks

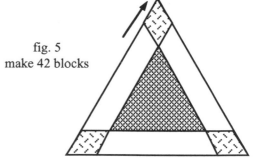

Arrange the blocks in six rows of seven blocks. See the quilt on page 21 for their positions.

Sew the blocks into horizontal rows. Press the seam allowances in the directions shown by the arrows in figure 6.

odd rows

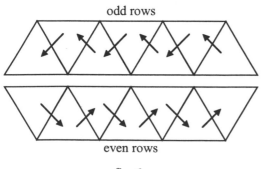

even rows

fig. 6

Add a side triangle which was cut from the 6 5/8" x 11 1/2" rectangles to the ends of each row. Press the seam allowances toward the side triangles. Trim the dog ears. Sew the rows together, carefully matching the seams and points of the diamonds. Press the seam allowances to one side.

Trim the selvage from the border fabric and cut four lengthwise panels (opposite of strip cutting) that are 4" wide (or wider, if desired). Attach these to the quilt using overlapped corners. See page 11 for more instruction on borders.

Options to Consider --

Twin, Full, or Queen Size

This quilt must always have an odd number of blocks in a row, and an even number of rows. Therefore, you may need to adjust the borders somewhat to get the fit you want on a bed size quilt. The bed sizes will require the following numbers of blocks:

Twin size   72 blocks (9 blocks x 8 rows)
Full size   88 blocks (11 blocks x 8 rows)
Queen size   80 blocks (13 blocks x 8 rows)

Table Runner

Perhaps because my class sample pieces are made in red and green, making a holiday table runner is a favorite project of the quilters in my workshops. Make two horizontal rows, each with seven or nine blocks. Eighteen blocks, two rows of nine blocks, will make a table runner that finishes approximately 20" x 54".

Debbie and her husband Dan as they were leaving Alaska for their new home in New Mexico.

About the Author

Debbie Caffrey is a self-published author of six books and eleven patterns. In addition, she has designed and published over ninety patterns in an ever-changing line of mystery quilts. Debbie has taught many energy-filled workshops nationwide for guilds and shops. These include Houston Quilt Festival, Minnesota Quilters' Conference, Festival of Classes in Bend, Oregon, and the Road to California. Debbie has contributed a number of articles to *Traditional Quiltworks* magazine and has appeared on two episodes of HGTV's television program, *Simply Quilts*.

Debbie and her husband Dan returned to the Middle Rio Grande Valley of New Mexico in the fall of 2000 where they live near the small community of La Joya. They had lived in Anchorage, Alaska, since 1979 where they raised their children Monica, Erin, and Mark. Besides quilting, Debbie enjoys long walks and drives and experiencing new places. In New Mexico Debbie and Dan spend many hours exploring the back roads and trails, watching the birds and animals, and studying the plants, rocks, and vistas of this diverse land.

Other books by Debbie Caffrey

Open a Can of Worms
Quilting Season
Scraps to You, Too
Blocks and Quilts Everywhere!
An Alaskan Sampler